# The Myth of The Jew in France
# 1967 - 1982

*to the memory of my PARENTS*

# The Myth of The Jew in France
# 1967 - 1982

## Henry H. Weinberg

*with a preface by*
*Robert Wistrich*
*(Professor of Modern Jewish History at the Hebrew University)*

**MOSAIC PRESS**
**Oakville — New York — London**

CANADIAN CATALOGUING IN PUBLICATION DATA

Weinberg, Henry H., 1935-
    The myth of the Jew in France, 1967-1982

Bibliography: p.
Includes index.
ISBN 0-88962-353-8 (bound) ISBN 0-88962-354-6 (pbk.)

1. Jews - France - History - 20th century.
2. Antisemitism - France - History - 20th century.
I. Title.

DS146.F73W44 1987     305.8'924'044     C87-094302-2

Published by Mosaic Press, P.O. Box 1032, Oakville, Ontario, L6J 5E9, Canada. Offices and warehouse at 1252 Speers Rd, Unit 10, Oakville, Ontario, L6L 5N9, Canada.

Published with the assistance of the Canada Council and the Ontario Arts Council.

Copyright ©Henry H. Weinberg, 1987
Design by Rita Vogel
Typesetting by Michael J. O'Leary
Printed and bound in Canada.

ISBN 0-88962-358-8 cloth
      0-88962-354-6 paper

MOSAIC PRESS:
**In the United States:**
    Riverrun Press Inc., 1170 Broadway, Suite 807, New York, N.Y., 10001, U.S.A..

**In the U.K.:**
    John Calder (Publishers) Ltd., 18 Brewer Street, London, W1R 4AS, England.

# CONTENTS

# Acknowledgments

My thanks go to the librarians at the Bibliothèque Nationale, the Centre de la Documentation Juive Contemporaine, the Bibliothèque de l'Alliance Israélite, and the Robarts Library of the University of Toronto. Sabine Roitman has supplied me with essential material from France and has arranged meetings with leaders in the French Jewish community.

Among the many people who have contributed to the writing of this book I am particularly grateful to Arnold Mandel for chats on the French-Jewish condition and attitudes to Jews in France. I am also indebted to the following individuals who discussed with me various aspects of the French-Jewish phenomenon: Jacques Amalric, the late Raymond Aron, Alain Besançon, François Debré, Charles Dreyfus, Alain Finkielkraut, Henri Hajdenberg, Lucien Klausner, Théo Klein, Annie Kriegel, Alain Peyrefitte, Roger Pierrot, Léon Poliakov, Jean-François Revel, the late Alain de Rothschild, Shimon Samuels, Laurence Soudet, Olivier Todd and Shmuel Trigano. The encouragement and advice of Robert Wistrich have been invaluable. Howard Aster and Frederick Krantz have made helpful suggestions. Ernie Mayer urged me to orient my scholarly activities to French Jewry. However, I alone am responsible for the views, errors and omissions contained in this book, as well as for most of the translations.

I am grateful to the editors of the following journals for permission to reprint segments of my articles: "French Jewry under the Mitterrand Presidency," *Contemporary French Civilization*, Vol. VIII (Fall-Winter, 1983-84), nos. 1-2; "French Jewry: Trauma and Renewal," *Midstream*, Vol. XXVIII (December, 1982), no. 10; "Le Monde and Israel," *Middle East Focus*, Vol. III (March, 1981), no. 6.

Grants from the Social Sciences and Humanities Research Council of Canada enabled me to conduct research in Paris.

My wife, Harriet, and my children, David, Eli, Deena and

Michael have, on more than one occasion served as a sounding board and have provided moral support. My Parisian friends, the Bierenbaums, the Grunbaums, the Hochsteins and the Silbers often gave me a home away from home. Last, but not least, Clara Stewart has deciphered the original manuscript and has patiently retyped subsequent versions. Her cheerful attitude and diligence facilitated the task. Lillian Lee worked with dedication on the final corrections.

# Preface

From the standpoint of modern Jewish history, France has always held a special position. The land of the Great Revolution of 1789, of the Rights of Man and the Enlightenment, was not surprisingly, the first European nation to fully emancipate the Jews. Nowhere else on the Continent was the Jewish minority so swiftly absorbed and socially integrated. Yet, already by the end of the 19th century, France was competing for top honours in the league table of European antisemitism. The Dreyfus Affair with its accompanying paroxysm of hatred and verbal violence directed at the small Jewish community, exposed unsuspected depths of Judeophobia which have led some historians to see in it a dress rehearsal for Nazism. In recent years, historical research has demonstrated the degree to which France was also a laboratory for the ideologies of "scientific" racism and an original, distinctive form of National Socialism. The extent of French collaboration with the Nazis under the Vichy régime underlines the importance of this independent tradition. The persistence and continuity of such traditions in the post-war era further suggests that antisemitic myths may well be more embedded in French culture and society than is commonly believed. Indeed, one might well ask which other European nation (with the exception of Germany) can vaunt so illustrious a literary legacy of antisemitism as that which extends from Voltaire and the Encylopaedists through Drumont, Barrès, Maurras to Bernanos, Drieu de la Rochelle and Giraudoux?

Nevertheless, the impact of the Holocaust and popular sympathy in the West (including France) for the newly created State of Israel, encouraged many to believe that anti-Jewish obsessions might become a thing of the past. For two decades a deceptive calm reigned on the surface until, in 1967, President Charles De Gaulle's notorious "sermon to the Hebrews" renewed the suspended debate on the "Jewish question". As Henry Weinberg shows in his thought-provoking and solidly documented book, it was as if a protective shield had been removed. Suddenly, the most impressive figure in modern French history, the symbol of its most cherished aspirations for freedom and national independence, was accusing not only the Israeli State but the Jewish people of arrogance, elitism and expansionist ambitions. Long-entrenched stereotypes about Jewish wealth, power and the urge to "dominate" resurfaced in the wake of Israel's spectacular victory and the General's unequivocal condemnation of its actions.

In retrospect, one must agree with Professor Weinberg, a new era of antisemitism had been inaugurated. Jewish criticism of the French government's pro-Arab policies quickly led in some Gaullist circles to charges of dual loyalty and insinuations that Jewish solidarity was incompatible with the security of the French State and its national interests.

De Gaulle's successors, Pompidou and Giscard d'Estaing continued this trend in their respective ways. Pompidou, in particular, displayed a growing antagonism towards Israel and its Jewish supporters in France and the United States. France increasingly voted with the Arabs at the United Nations, blamed Israel for the oil crisis and created difficulties for it in the European Economic Community. Under Giscard, assistance was provided for Iraq's nuclear programme, close ties were established with oil-rich Arab States and official French flirtations with Arafat paved the way for legitimizing the PLO in the eyes of Western public opinion. One of the more disastrous consequences of this policy was a new laxity and tolerance toward Middle Eastern terrorist organizations, symbolized by the French release in 1977 of Abu Daoud, who had masterminded the Olympic Games massacre of Israeli athletes five years earlier. Today, France is reaping the whirlwind as Paris has been turned into a battleground for a complex myriad of Arab terrorist groups.

Henry Weinberg's book convincingly documents the mechanisms through which such policies also encouraged a lifting of post-Holocaust taboos on the public expression of antisemitism in France. Since the late 1960s a parallel development on the French Left reinforced the official trend. The French Communist Party (a much more powerful force at the time than it has since become) expressed its "solidarity" with the Palestinians by vituperative denunciations of Israeli "imperialism" and world Zionism. True to its Stalinist traditions it presented Israel not only as an aggressive, militarist State and agent of American interests but linked its nefarious role on the world stage to the machinations of international Jewish bankers. The antisemitic tone of some of its propaganda fused older patterns of 19th century socialist Judeophobia in France with totalitarian amalgams derived from the Soviet Stalinist arsenal. Not surprisingly, it has been one of the major purveyors in France of the canard that Zionism is a form of racism and Israel a post-war reincaranation of the Third Reich.

Such rhetorical excesses were also a commonplace of the many *gauchiste* sects which flourished in France during the decade which followed the Six Day War. More extreme than the Communists, their commitment to the "liberation of Palestine" explicitly envisaged the destruction or "dismantling" of the Jewish State. This leftist anti-Zionism (best qualified as the anti-imperialism of fools) generally went hand in hand with an anti-racism which perversely excluded the Jews from the doubtful benefits of its compassion. Indeed, as the author of these lines can testify from personal experience, the old cry of *"Mort aux Juifs!"* (once the preserve of the French Right) was more than once to be heard at extreme left demonstrations against Israel in the early 1970s. The authentic offspring of this pro-Palestinian *gauchisme*, the *Action Directe* of the 1980s, has long since extended the circle of its attention beyond Jewish or Zionist targets to the overthrow of French democracy itself.

The visceral racism and antisemtism of the Neo-Nazi Right in France, which had never altogether disappeared in the post-war years, also found encouragement in the new climate of suspicion toward Jews engendered in the 1970s. In contrast to the extreme Left, their racism was uninhibited and able to feed on a real social problem, the growing hostility of the French population to North African Arab immigrants. The scale of this immigration and the xenophobia it engendered has provided the basis for the spectacular rise of Europe's strongest neo-fascist movement, the *Front National* led by Le Pen. Its rhetoric of *La France aux Français*, while officially eschewing explicit and blatant antisemitism, recalls the traditions of Drumont and Maurras as well as the fascist leagues of the 1930s. Between the lines of its assaults on prominent French politicians of Jewish origin like Simone Veil and Robert Badinter one can easily detect the time-honoured themes of the radical French Right for whom the Jews are as always, a "colonizing" power in France.

No less disturbing for French Jews is the preoccupation of the

Right with the so-called Holocaust hoax (which has also found more than a few echoes on the extreme Left). In its efforts to clean up the image of Nazi crimes and thereby to rehabilitate the fascist legacy, the French Right has not hesitated to disseminate the monstrous lie that the murder of six million Jews was a deliberately fabricated myth serving the interests of Israel. Similar charges have been made by neo-Nazis throughout the Western world and sponsored or subsidized by Arab money. But in France the new "revisionism" has found a particularly fertile terrain, encouraged by advocates like Professor Robert Faurisson and providing the subject for a university dissertation along similar lines that was initially approved by the academic authorities. Professor Weinberg skilfully establishes the historic context which has made such crackpot fantasies respectable in certain circles. The scandalous interview with the unrepentant Nazi, Darquier de Pellepoix, in the mass-circulation L'Express (1978), la mode rétro in the French cinema during the 1970s, the fascination with the SS, the Gestapo and the Vichy period, the publication of memoirs by former French fascists, the rediscovery of Céline, etc. all contributed in their different ways to the erosion of certain taboos. A former Pétain admirer, Alfred Fabre-Luce could impudently revive some of the oldest clichés about the Jews (claiming they had always brought persecution down on their own heads) and be granted a respectful hearing.

As Weinberg shows, this intellectual climate that accompanied the closing years of Giscard D'Estaing's regime (with its suggestive echoes of the Vichy past) turned antisemitism into just another political opinion. Against this background, the assassinations of Henri Curiel (1978) and Pierre Goldman (1979), the flurry of antisemitic graffiti on Paris subway walls, the growing number of terror attacks against Jewish targets in France, the harassment of Jewish students and the desecration of cemeteries appear less suprising. Henry Weinberg's book makes us understand that the assault on the liberal synagogue in the Rue Copernic (1980)—seen as a turning-point by many French Jews—did not come out of the blue. It was the logical climax of more than a decade of subtle incitement and official laxity which sought to isolate French Jews and make them stand apart from other Frenchmen. Suddenly, with the clarity of an X-ray photograph, the precarity of the Jewish community in France stood revealed in all its nakedness, heightened by the cool reaction of the Government and police ineptitude in uncovering the perpetrators.

Not the least of Weinberg's merits is the skill with which he exposes the complicities of the "progressive" intelligentsia in preparing (unwittingly no doubt) the ground for a new antisemitism. In a penetrating chapter on *Le Monde* which will doubtless raise many eyebrows, he dissects the techniques by which it pursued a long campaign of psychological warfare against the Jewish State under the mask of a high-minded objectivity. This campaign of disinformation, infinitely more effective than that of the Communists, with its use of emotionally loaded terms like *occupation*, *résistance* and *repression* to discredit and blacken Israel's image, was not without consequences. This was not merely a question of *le tiers-mondisme*, so fashionable in France, with its built-in anti-American and anti-Zionist ideological bias, but a campaign that called in doubt the loyalties of French Jews no less insistently than had successive Gaullist governments. Moreover, whenever it was accused of flirting with antisemitism, *Le Monde* could always point to its gallery of anti-Zionist Jews to proclaim its virginal innocence. Yet the same *Le Monde* did not hesitate to publish Faurisson or Jean-Marie Paupert's diatribe against French Jews, maliciously suggesting that they should know their place and refrain from persecuting and manipulating Frenchmen! Hostility to Israel, as Weinberg convincingly demonstates, ineluctably slides into the murky waters of anti-Jewish prejudice.

Nothing illustrates this process more clearly than the French media antagonism towards the Jews and Israel in the wake of the Lebanon war of 1982. For a few months, at the height of the hostilities, it appeared as if a new witchhunt was in progress. Wild accusations about the "genocide" of the Palestinian people were rampant across the French political spectrum. Communists, Trotskyists, left-wing Socialists, Gaullists, "progressive" Catholics, pro-Palestinian and Arab intellectuals all added their voices to that of *Le Monde*, which reprovingly wrote of "le fascisme aux couleurs d'Israël". Israelis were branded as Nazis, hoary Christian clichés about Old Testament fanaticism and the tribal-racist character of Judaism found a new lease on life. Where are these great humanitarians today, as Syria crushes Lebanon in its iron grip and Shi'ites remorselessly starve the Palestinian camps into submission?

Professor Weinberg evokes the anguish of French Jewry in the wake of this media assault and the deadly terrorist attack on Goldenberg's delicatessen in the old Jewish quarter of Paris. He is also careful to point out the limits to the progress of antisemitism in France, though the point might have been elaborated upon at greater length. France is not, after all, an antisemitic State. Not only is there full Jewish equality but the success of French Jews in virtually all areas of French life has been impressive, even astounding in some respects. Catholic efforts to eradicate Judeophobia have been sincere and contributed much to an erosion of the old religiously-based antagonism to Jews and Judaism. François Mitterrand since his accession to the Presidency in 1981 has confirmed what his past record already suggested—that his empathy and understanding for the Jewish people is equal, if not superior to that of any major French political leader in the past. Public opinion polls (Weinberg regards them with some scepticism) also suggest a diminution in the intensity of popular antisemitism, though in a country as volatile and rife with political passion as France, such data are unpredictable and sudden changes may easily occur. What sense is one to make then of the public events and intellectual trends influencing French attitudes to the Jews in the period described by this book and in the immediate present?

Part of the answer is revealed in Weinberg's last chapter, which though somewhat sketchy and impressionistic, points to a profound and important mutation in the self-consciousness of French Jewry. The hostility to Israel and the reopening of a "Jewish question" in France, he suggests, has provoked by way of paradoxical response, a reawakening of interest in Judaism, a greater concern for Israel and sensitivity to antisemitism. There has been a reassessment of the old assimilationist ideology that survived the Dreyfus Affair and even the trauma of Vichy. Unconditional loyalty to France no longer seems in the 1980s to provide protection against physical or verbal threats. Traditional ideologies of French republican patriotism or secular Marxist universalism have become anachronistic and unacceptable, especially if they are to be bought at the expense of Jewish identity. Nor is the submissiveness of the established communal leadership to the French State appropriate to the new situation. The reign of the notables, symbolized by the Rothschild hegemony in communal affairs, is finally over.

What has replaced it is a new style of political activism, a new Jewish militancy and assertiveness represented by organizations like *le Renouveau Juif*. Many French Jews are no longer afraid of manifesting their particularism. They no longer fear the charge of dual loyalty or at times to act as an organized political pressure group even if this entails a conflict with government policy. In place of the *Juif honteux* we have a new pride in Jewishness. They no longer wish to disappear as Jews but rather to affirm their solidarity and commitment to Israel and with other Jewish communities outside France. The Frenchman "of the Mosaic persuasion" and even the *Israélite* of 19th century vintage, is a declining species, though he may yet account for a third of the Jewish population in France.

Weinberg's explanation for this mutation involves multiple factors though he links it dialectically with the antisemitic pressures of the French environment since 1967. He attributes a decisive influence to Israel (somewhat excessive in my view) seeing in its bravado and model of the fighting Jew standing up for his independence, an inspirational example for the reassertion of a positive Jewish identity. Certainly, since 1967, the traditional coolness of French Jews towards Zionism (which as far back as 1897 prompted Theodor Herzl to write them off as potential adherents to the cause) has faded and the commitment of the community to Israel runs deep. But many of the signs of revitalization in French Judaism to which the author himself points, suggest that Zionism may only have been a catalyst which leads off in other directions. Thus the renewal of interest in Yiddish, in the Sephardi heritage and folklore, the turn from Marx and Mao to the Talmud and Cabala, the greater observance of *kashrut*, the impact of the Lubavitcher Hassidim, and the neo-Diasporism of some French-Jewish intellectuals are scarcely marks of a Zionist renaissance in France. They testify to a significant thirst for Jewish authenticity and the rediscovery of Jewish roots which transcend a Zionist ideology that may have less appeal to French-Jewish youth than the author assumes.

The return to traditional Jewish texts in the writings of intellectuals like Lévinas, Trigano or even at a more popular level of Bernard-Henri Lévy, represents perhaps the search for an authentic Jewish message, long distorted by Western Christendom and by secular emancipationist ideologies which alienated French Jews from their own heritage. Such a search will necessarily entail a critique of Zionism whose political philosophy is predicated on the same Jacobin nation-state model which is being reassessed in France.

Weinberg rightly points to the impact on the French Jewish community of the Maghrebin immigration in the 1960s. The Jewish immigration from North Africa transformed the demographic, socio-economic and cultural profile of French Jewry beyond recognition and it is probably too early to assess its full impact. The greater assertiveness of French Jews and their emotional solidarity with Israel clearly owes much to this immigration. Its influence on communal institutions, attitudes and intellectual trends is much less clear as is its effect on French perceptions of Jewry. Unlike the East European Jewish immigrants between the wars, the North African Jews were already acculturated and not subjected to the xenophobic backlash of earlier generations of newcomers. Moreover their Jewish identity had a stronger basis in religious tradition, in family ties and the experience of Mediterranean societies only superficially touched by the secularizing influences of modernity. How long they are likely to resist the assimilationist pull of French society and culture, given current rates of intermarriage and the endemic weakness of Jewish communal structures in France, must remain an open question.

Nevertheless as Weinberg poings out, there are some grounds for hope as well as vigilance. The monolithic, centralist structure of French society is slowing crumbling, for reason altogether unconnected with the Jewish presence. The revival of regionalist and ethnic identities (Basque, Breton, Occitans, Corsican etc.), the more pluralist character of French culture today and the recognition by the government of le droit à la différence have probably favoured the growing wish to assert a distinctive Jewish identity. They may have further accelerated the sense of French Jews that assimilation as it was understood in the 19th century is a cul-de-sac. Gone are the days when the Israélites of France naively believed that "the time of the Messiah had arrived with the French Revolution"; gone, too, is the time when the majority of French Jews could hope with Theodore Reinach that having delivered its message, Judaism "could die without regrets, buried in its triumphs". What exactly will replace the mirage of total assimilation is as yet unclear but gives rise to a cautious optimism concerning the creative potential of a vibrant Jewish community still in the process of becoming. Henry Weinberg's perceptive study captures both the anguish and the promise of this community at a crucial moment of transition.

*Robert Wistrich*
*Visiting Professor*
*École des Hautes Études en Sciences Sociales*

*Paris*
*March 1987*

# Introduction

Since the final decades of the nineteenth century the "Jewish question" has played a significant role in the cultural, social and political life of France. In spite of the fact that France was, until the 1930s, home to one of the smallest concentrations of Jews in Europe, the emergence of modern France, its political and socio-economic struggles, even its cultural debates, have been linked to the presence of Jews in its midst. The belief that France's welfare and future orientation was deeply affected by this presence was fostered by political theorists, publicists and novelists. In spite of transformations in both individual and corporate perceptions of nationalism in recent years, in spite of changes in French attitudes to Jews, the obsession with the myth of the Jew was has not vanished. A prominent historian has written recently that, "the fate of the Jews in France has become a touchstone for our understanding modern French history as a whole." Patrice Higonnet underscored the fact that "anti-Semitism has become a critical representation of some fundamental aspects of French culture."[1] A literary critic, who has used a "deconstructionist" critical approach in studying Judeophobia in French literature, has claimed that anti-Semitism "at times appears to be the medium of French cultural achievement at its most characteristic."[2]

From Fourier in the 1830s to Céline a century later, important French thinkers, writers and journalists disseminated a variety of notions about Jews that would be used to alleviate fears and frustrations and to sooth the pain of nostalgia for past glories. Judeophobia also served as a rationalization and, in periods of flux and transition, as a consensus builder in the face of threats to social, political and economic stability. The Dreyfus Affair became a political battle ground and a source of national trauma. At the same time, Marcel Proust's novels show that anti-Dreyfus sentiment served to bring together aristocracy and the lower classes.

In rare moments of accord both right and left-wing ideologists have expounded notions of social reform based on hostility to Jews. Even in periods of relative social calm the preoccupation with the mystery represented by the Jewish people remained intense. In the words of the historian, Theodor Zeldin, anti-Semitism has been a "constant of French passions."

It has been pointed out that throughout history, Jews "have been persecuted for believing in Judaism and excoriated for disbelieving; despised when poor and loathed when rich; shamed for their ignorance of the host culture and rebuffed for mastering it; denounced as capitalists and assailed as Communists; derided for their separation and reviled for their assimilation."[3] There have been many attempts to define this astonishing phenomenon. The definitions have touched on political, psychological and moral elements. It has been called a political neurosis and collective psychopathology, a tool of the right and the left to buttress totalitarianism, and both a moral monstrosity and intellectual nonsense.

In the preface to his seminal work on the myth of a Jewish conspiracy to dominate the world, Norman Cohn points out that the term, myth, can take on several meanings. It can signify a false belief, a credo which generates a sense of mission, and also an "imaginative construction" which allows a people to define the world around it.[4] All three definitions seem to fit aptly the function of the anti-Jewish phenomenon in modern France. Although researchers have found that many aspects of anti-Semitism are not directly linked to the presence or to the perceived behavior of Jews—Sartre saw it as a fear of the human condition and as a paradigm of universal reality[5]—particular traditions and social-psychological structures do explain its fertility on French soil. It is significant that Jeanne d'Arc, the archetypal French national heroine, has been used as a symbol to whip up anti-Jewish sentiment.[6] Some students of French anti-Semitism have gone as far as to claim that it represents a "Weltanschauung", a "philosophy" of French society, "an entire architecture."[7] This hyperbole does not negate the fact that anti-liberalism, racism and xenophobia often found their expression on French soil clothed in anti-Semitic rhetoric. It has been demonstrated that French thinkers created "the intellectual matrix" for European Fascism[8] and that the modern concept of race was in great measure elaborated in France.

Yet it seems paradoxical that the nation which was the first to grant emancipation to the Jews in Europe, which often symbolized high political ideals, which fought with itself over the guilt or innocence of a Jewish army officer, should be tainted with the stigma of abject racism. And, indeed, some historians have gone to great lengths to avoid charging the French with Judeophobia. Evidently, the hermeneutics of French anti-Semitism mobilizes strong feelings; "it is problematical, hard to live with, and hard to reconcile with one's emotions."[9] The author of a major study on twentieth-century France has even managed to discuss the Dreyfus Affair without mentioning the fact that Dreyfus was a Jew.[10]

It is undeniable, however, that France played a central role in the elaboration of modern anti-Semitism. For some of the great figures of the French Enlightenment—among them Voltaire, who somehow managed to be both a defender of human rights and an anti-Semite—the Jews were the "great witnesses of the errors of the established religion."[11] Soon after the 1791 Constituent Assembly's decree emancipating the Jews, the enemies of the Revolution began to single out the Jews as its main beneficiaries. The rapid accession of French Jews to professions denied to them before the Revolution engendered accusations of exploitation and domination. If, before the Revolution, Jews were excoriated as the initiators of the Catholic religion, after it, they were charged with atheism, or were branded as the enemies of Christianity. The philosopher, Joseph de Maistre, linked even Napoleon to a Jewish conspiracy.[12] Among Jacobins, the accusation that the Jews constituted a nation within a nation echoed with particular force.

By the middle of the nineteenth century French Jews had reached a degree of integration into the general society unequalled elsewhere in Europe. Some Jewish financiers — whose importance is reflected already in Balzac's fiction in the 1830s — had become leaders in advancing modernization. Using bankers as models of the greedy Jew, serious thinkers, such as Alphonse de Toussenel, were busy drafting the blueprint of a modern political anti-Semitism that would lead to the Dreyfus Affair. Conservatives saw the Jews as the proponents of change and progress, while Socialists blamed them as the promoters of capitalism. The Socialist, Joseph Proudhon, reflected the degree of hostility to Jews in his camp. He urged that they be either "sent back to Asia," or "exterminated."

The humiliations of the Franco-Prussian war, the political

wranglings that followed it, and a series of financial collapses and scandals blamed on Jews —and echoed in the fiction of such prominent writers as Zola, Maupassant and Bourget — made French opinion ripe for a skillful demagogue who would establish anti-Semitism as "the philosophy of French modernity."[13] In his bestselling *La France juive* (1886), Edouard Drumont tried to establish a connection between the recovery of France from the consequences of the Franco-Prussian war and its ridding itself of the Jews. Drumont, who represented the link between Catholic and Socialist anti-Semitism, singled out the enemy: the Jewish, capitalist and anti-Catholic Republic. Drumont also focused on the Jew in mirroring French anxieties vis-a-vis modernity. The myth of a Jewish conspiracy against France helped to exorcise and to rationalize the dreaded evils of the modern age.

From the early 1880s on, a new literary genre, the anti-Semitic novel, acquired considerable popularity. Novels in which the Jew was portrayed as an immoral intruder and a rapacious parasite became best-sellers. One publisher alone, Savine, printed more than fifty anti-Semitic titles in a seven year period. Literary anti-Semitism became a means of explaining the misfortunes of French life. Fiction served as an instrument for stimulating anti-Jewish activity.

The Dreyfus Affair represents the first successful use of anti-Semitism as a political weapon in an attempt to overthrow a republican regime. The fate of French democracy was linked to the fate of an obscure Jewish artillery officer. It was also the first time that an anti-Jewish campaign was whipped up, not against the "uncivilized," unkempt ghetto Jew, but against the most assimilated Jewry in Europe. Yet the outcome of the Dreyfus case, with its epic dimensions of poetic justice, engendered the hope that France would cease to be roused by anti-Semitic emotion. The involvement of a substantial segment of public opinion on behalf of a Jew, symbolized by the magnificent courage of Emile Zola — whose intervention in the "Affaire" was aptly eulogized as "a moment in the conscience of mankind" — led many to believe that anti-Semitism had lost its appeal for the French people.

The appearance of right-wing anti-Semitism at the turn of the century under the banner of the influential movement, "Action Française," soon controverted the impression that a radical change in attitudes had occurred. Under the leadership of Charles Maurras, a writer who would be elected to the "Académie Française," this movement echoed many of Drumont's themes of

Jewish villainy in the name, this time, of a royalist ideology. Maurras, who fascinated many personalities in the twentieth century — among them Charles De Gaulle—claimed that the "providential arrival" of anti-Semitism was crucial to his political success. For almost three decades, until the late 1920s, "Action Française," which drew to its ranks some brilliant writers, was highly conspicuous in French political life.

By the 1930s, anti-Semitism had achieved wide social acceptance. It turned into an emotional climate that touched both intellectuals and the masses. It set a tone that affected perceptions and sensibilities. For many French intellectuals Jewishness "became a code-term for a category of destruction, at once horrifying and fascinating."[14] Blind Jew-hatred inspired the writings of a literary genius, Céline, and fatefully desensitized minds to the evil that was to follow, under Vichy. There is little doubt that in a country where literature has traditionally been held in the highest esteem, literary anti-Semitism furnished the professional anti-Semites with considerable intellectual sanction. The myth of the Jewish conspiracy was revived by a major writer, Georges Bernanos, who in his *La Grande peur des biens-pensants* (1936), took it upon himself to restore the influence of Drumont's anti-Semitic thought. The Jewish origins of the leader of the "Front Populaire," Léon Blum, were fully exploited by his political rivals.

For some writers the "Jewish question" became again a literary theme. In the novel, *Gilles*, by the influential novelist and publicist, Drieu de la Rochelle, the Jew incarnates the modern world, which stands in opposition to all the qualities embodied in traditional France. Even literary critics indulged in promoting Jew-hatred. In 1937, the critic, Thierry Maulnier, reprinted in his monthly, *Combat*, excerpts from the works of Drumont and Maurras. Maurice Blanchot, the critic whose work is central to twentieth-century French criticism, decried the "betrayal" of France by "revolutionaries and Jews."[15] In the openly anti-Semitic *Pleins pouvoirs*, the acclaimed playwright, Jean Giraudoux, warned against the invasion of France by the "hordes" from "Polish and Roumanian ghettos." Bernanos, an opponent of fascism, reproached Hitler for having "discredited forever" the term, anti-Semitism.

Sartre told in poignant terms the depth of the stigma of being Jewish in France in the 1930s' by describing the trauma of a Jewish child's discovery of his Jewishness: "some day they must discover the truth: from the smiles of those who surround them, from the rumor and the insults . . . they return home, they look at their father, they think: 'Is he a Jew too?' and the respect they had for him is poisoned."[16] The pervasiveness of the scorn and hatred toward Jews in the pre-war years was not without consequences. Three months after Hitler's troops marched into Paris, Pétain's government promulgated anti-Jewish statutes on its own initiative. The massive collaboration of the French authorities in the deportation of Jews to Auschwitz remains one of the darkest moments in recent French history.

In the years following the end of World War II several signs pointed to a desire on the part of the French to liquidate their anti-Semitic past. Jews were, after all, the victims of the greatest organized mass murder in history and the French bore guilt for the deportation of 100,000 Jews from their territory. Although it met with reservations from some circles, the establishment of a Jewish state, in 1948, aroused popular sympathy. The tacit military alliance between France and Israel until the end of the war in Algeria was based not only on political and economic factors; it also enjoyed the emotional approval of a majority of the French people.

The period of cooperation between France and Israel came to a halt when President De Gaulle decided to take advantage of the June, 1967, Arab-Israeli war to change French foreign policy in the Middle East. Having settled the painful and disruptive war in Algeria De Gaulle resolved to mend fences with the Arab world in the name of "traditional ties," but above all for pragmatic reasons: a reinvigorated industry was eager for new markets. The French President confided to one of his ministers, Alain Peyrefitte, that a potential market, a hundred-fold larger than Israel's, warranted a reorientation of policy.

De Gaulle did not only make gestures of friendship toward the Arabs; at a press conference, in November, 1967, he attacked Israel using rhetoric that was perceived by many to be anti-Semitic. The distinguished scholar, Raymond Aron, charged that De Gaulle "authorized a new anti-Semitism."[17] Because of De Gaulle's comments on Israel, Aron added, "state anti-Semitism became again *salonfähig*."[18] Aron also deplored the fact that such literary giants as François Mauriac and André Malraux, who were close to De Gaulle, did not react to what he considered as the opening of a new era of anti-Semitism.

De Gaulle's anti-Israeli policies merged with other seemingly unrelated factors to produce a rash of verbal and at times physical hostility toward French Jewry. A highly-publicized re-examination of the Vichy period, a new curiosity about Judaism and the constant debates over the Arab-Israeli conflict, brought the Jewish phenomenon into the limelight. In the name of the public's "right to know" respectable journalists dug up old anti-Semitic material and presented it as an intellectual discovery. Some newspapers, following in De Gaulle's footsteps, failed to draw the line between criticism of Israeli policies and the Jewish "character" that allegedly motivated them.

After the bombing of a Paris synagogue in 1980, one of the most respected political figures in France, Simone Veil, charged that the government's policies blurred distinctions between hostility to Israel and anti-Jewish sentiment: "when ambiguity is allowed to float; when some anti-Israeli attacks are in fact anti-Semitic, when one mixes such a policy with the situation of Jews in France, one creates anti-Semitism."[19]

Although in the 1970s France was not alone to court the oil-rich Arab world, it was particularly quick to cater to its Arab clients, to align itself, more than any other European state, with their hostile policies toward Israel. In the United Nations, the French representative often defended the Arab cause and France regularly endorsed one-sided resolutions condemning Israeli preemptive actions against terrorists. The French government also struck secret deals with Arab terrorists, allowing them to use its territory in exchange for exempting French targets from their attacks. At least as far back as the mid 1970s, during the administration of Valéry Giscard d'Estaing, France negotiated agreements with terrorists.

When the gunmen broke the understanding, French Jews became their first victims. Later, non-Jewish Frenchmen also became the casualties of the government's ill-fated scheme. The new policy on the Middle East affected French Jews in other ways. To comply with the Arab trade boycott of Israel, French authorities exceeded at times the requirements of the Arabs and allowed discrimination against Jewish citizens on France's own soil. In intellectual circles and on campuses the image of the Israeli soldier was assimilated to that of the brutal French paratrooper in Algeria, and Israel was labeled a bridgehead of Western imperialism.

The government-controlled television and radio fostered sympathy for the Palestinians and leveled harsh criticism at Israel. Moreover, French Jewry's support for Israel, and particularly its critique of the new Middle Eastern policy, drew accusations of disloyalty from government spokesmen. De Gaulle and his advisers failed to distinguish between traditional French notions of loyalty and the sentimental support for one of the most daring enterprises of recent history: the merger of an ancient belief and of a modern ideological aspiration. Spurred on by the assertive and proud North-African Jews (who by the 1970s constituted a majority), community organizations issued statements forthright in their defense of Zionism. Stunned by open attacks on them by high officials, insulted by a palpable legitimation of anti-Semitic rhetoric, the Jews also expressed deep concern. In 1978 Pierre Goldman, the author of a moving autobiography on his life as a "Polish Jew born in France," wrote that French Jews rediscovered that "nothing is yet settled" about their status in France. By 1979, a series of extended interviews with a cross-section of French Jewry, *Juifs et Français*, revealed that "the feeling of insecurity was unanimous; it was felt as a silent, latent and constant threat."[20] The authors of *Juifs et Français* speculated whether France might again become "unliveable" for Jews.

That same year, a well-known Paris intellectual accused the Jews of fabricating their own vengeful version of their mistreatment by the Vichy regime. Alfred Fabre-Luce urged Jews to adopt a "lower profile" and to abandon their support for Israel. He also conjured up a conspiracy of historians, most of them Jewish, to rewrite French history.[21] Fabre-Luce proved that the old-style anti-Semitism can still exist in the post-Holocaust era. Reinforcing this notion, a regular *Le Monde* columnist, Philippe de Saint-Robert, wrote that Israel was the "metropolis of an elusive and omnipresent empire." The old myth of world Jewish domination was back under a new guise. *Le Monde's* consistently anti-Israeli editorial line seemed to authorize occasional anti-Semitic outbursts by some of its contributors. After the appearance of a particularly offensive, clearly anti-Semitic article on the front page of *Le Monde*, the novelist, Simone de Beauvoir, Sartre's life-long companion, charged the Paris newspaper with a long-standing anti-Jewish bias. The Paris daily used even its professed liberal orientation to attack the Jewish state: "*Le Monde* was among the pioneers in Western highbrow journalism of the technique of turning public revulsion against anti-Semitism and Nazism, into a stick with which to beat Israel."[22]

France also became the only Western democracy where Jews were warned on the pages of prestigious newspapers that they faced dire consequences unless they refrained from supporting their reborn ancestral homeland, and stopped reproving government policy on the Middle East. France was also unique in that the Middle Eastern policies of right-of-centre administrations were backed by the left; the powerful Communist Party, some Socialists, left-wing Catholics and the influential, predominently leftist intelligentsia. Anti-Zionism, often tinged with Judeophobia, became a frequent theme in the high-circulation press controlled by the leftists. Soviet propaganda, which already in the 1960s identified Zionism with colonialism, found a receptive audience in the French left. Its espousal of such a fabrication evoked disturbing memories, and, according to some, stemmed from the fact that the French left lacked the intellectual tools to analyse the reality of the situation. It conceptualized its attitude to Israel and its Jewish supporters in terms of colonialism and imperialism, and the "old tools of the French political culture...above all, a latent anti-Semitism."[23]

Although Sartre, the mentor of the intellectual left, stated, in 1977, that some forms of anti-Zionism were indeed anti-Semitic, many of his followers seemed to disregard the warning. Léon Poliakov, the eminent historian of anti-Semitism, declared that the difference between anti-Semitism and anti-Zionism, "if it exists," is at best "razor thin." Another historian wrote that the word "Zionist" is very convenient for anti-Semites, because it is "charged with all the sins of Israel, with the famous forgery, *The Protocols of the Elders of Zion*, and permits the displacement of the term, anti-Semitism."[24] Since, in the post-Holocaust era, direct expression of hostility to Jews became unacceptable to the majority of Western public opinion, the term, anti-Zionism, furnished a new rhetorical mutation, in which the alleged target was no longer a people, but an ideology. Nevertheless, anti-Zionist propaganda utilized the traditional images and metaphors of anti-Semitism. In the eyes of some anti-Zionists the creation of the State of Israel seems to have merely added the dimension of statehood to the "Jewish question."

Like the opponents of Israel elsewhere, French anti-Zionists argued that their political stance did not reflect an anti-Jewish attitude. And indeed, it is perhaps possible to be a non-Zionist, oppose policies of the Jewish state and advocate the assimilation of Jews without being anti-Semitic. Anti-Zionists have resorted, however, "to every conceivable distortion and ideological absurdity... to explain why only Zionism among national liberation movements is *illegitimate* and ultimately condemned to extinction."[25]

French anti-Zionism also manifested itself on the right. Historical "revisionists" of the Holocaust claimed that Hitler's gas chambers were invented by Zionists in order to legitimize the establishment of Israel. An elitist right-wing think tank, the "Nouvelle Droite," denounced "metaphysical" Judaism in the name of a return, to Aryan, European roots. A small but vociferous neo-Nazi movement, centered in the University of Paris Faculty of Law, resorted to violence in the name of a similar ideology. Other neo-Nazi groups perpetrated attacks on Jews and Jewish communal buildings, provoking fear and consternation. Although the perpetrators of an attack on a Paris synagogue in 1980 (which resulted in four dead and over twenty wounded), were never caught, a right-wing organization took credit. According to the authoritative Institute of Jewish Affairs in London, 62% of all anti-Jewish acts of violence in Europe, from 1980 to 1985, occurred in France. (There were 154 attacks in 16 countries. Of these, 73% were against Jewish institutions and individuals; the rest against Israeli targets).[26]

The effects of the anti-Israeli pronouncements over a fifteen-year period culminated in unprecedented hostility toward Jews during the 1982 war in Lebanon. Jewish students in French high schools were treated as accomplices of Israel's "crimes" and major segments of the media sanctioned the open expression of hatred toward Jews. The discussion was not just about Israel and Zionism, but "a major debate over the nature of Judaism was inaugurated."[27] Le Monde, Libération, and the Catholic weekly, Témoignage Chrétien, were sued by human-rights organizations for defamation and incitement to racial hatred. The philosopher Alain Finkielkraut, referring to De Gaulle's 1967 press conference, wrote fifteen years later: "Thus De Gaulle won. His 1967 phrase, 'a self-assured, domineering, elite people'...which created a scandal at the time, came to full fruition during the war in Lebanon. The significance of this success calls for reflection."[28] After years of slanted coverage of the Middle East conflict came blatant expressions of Judeophobia. The 1982 war also demonstrated that even free media could prove to be "as vulnerable to the wooden language of propaganda as a censured press."[29]

The noted French historian, François Furet, expressed concern that "the international existence of the State of Israel involves the Diaspora in solidarities that are probably universalizing a return to anti-Semitism in a form and on a scale that are unprecedented."[30] Yet some academics have discounted the seriousness of contemporary anti-Semitism and have implied that it is on the way to extinction. They have gone to great lengths to deny that Judeophobia is a historical phenomenon and that there is anything distinctive, or unique, about it.[31]

Both on historical and objective grounds such a position is untenable. A possible explanation for the advocacy of this specious view lies in the wishful thought that Jews since Emancipation, have fully integrated into Western society, no longer constitute an exceptional Diaspora, and that therefore today, the Jewish condition is indistinguishable from the general human condition. Moreover, because anti-Semitism globally has become a predominently left-wing and Third World phenomenon, leftist intellectuals have had difficulty conceptualizing its nature, and have become reluctant to admit its existence or gravity. It is also possible that some, along with Sartre in the 1940s, still believe that a more just, Socialist society would bring about the demise of Judeophobia. Events of the last decades have hardly provided any new evidence to substantiate such notions which, at best, fail to account for the irrational element in anti-Semitism and for the fact that some myths "do not necessarily disappear with the circumstances that first produced them."[32]

Although prominent sociologists have expressed grave doubts about the validity of survey research — Theodor Adorno has called it "thoroughly superficial and misguided" and Gunnar Myrdal doubted its impartiality — some observers have pointed to opinion polls as significant indicators of a decrease in hostility to Jews, disregarding their questionable value, particularly in estimating the depth of anti-Semitism.[33] A psychological phenomenon as knotty as anti-Semitism is not given to meaningful analysis through unsophisticated polling methods, often reduced to a single focus. Lucy Dawidowicz, the author of a definitive study on the Holocaust, has expressed great reservations about the validity of polls which try to "measure" anti-Semitism: "Survey analysis at its best, free from intrusive politics, is, with its simple focus on opinion, not properly geared to the etiology of anti-Semitism. Useful for periodic pulse-taking, it nevertheless serves ultimately to limit our understanding of anti-Semitism, which is a phenomenon marked by a high degree of multiformity and contradictoriness."[34] Thus, both the validity and the relevance of polls in gauging anti-Semitism would appear to be highly questionable, especially in a country like France whose modern history has witnessed its multifaceted appearance in varied circumstances at frequent intervals.

A French commentator has observed that in opinion polls, those who do not wish to take responsibility for revealing their true sentiments, attribute them obliquely to others, and that anti-Semitism "often takes the detour of 'noticing' the existence of hostility to Jews," rather than manifesting itself openly.[35] The display of anti-Semitic tendencies during the war in Lebanon showed, according to Yehuda Bauer, that anti-Semitism, "is *never* far below the surface" and that the "relevant opinion polls must be reexamined with great care."[36] Referring to the polls showing a decline in popular anti-Semitism, Bauer wrote that it is possible to generalize from the Nazi experience that "extreme anti-Semitism does not require extreme anti-Semitic convictions in the mass of the population."[37]

The French-Jewish philosopher, Shmuel Trigano, has stated recently that "the socio-political and ideological structure which supports anti-Semitism in France is intact, powerful and unflagging...."[38] The anti-Semitic bias in the French media during the 1982 war in Lebanon was seen as a confirmation of this view.[39] However, France cannot be labelled an overtly anti-Semitic state today. It is not on the verge of a violent, popular anti-Jewish eruption and its official treatment of Jews has not been noticeably worse than that of other Western societies. The mainstream Catholic Church in France has made considerable efforts to eradicate the more salient aspects of Judeophobia in its liturgy, and President Mitterrand's genuine empathy with the Jewish people has no doubt affected public opinion. Yet the ingredients for a dangerous change in the status are present. The cultural and historical roots of French attitudes to Jews add to this fact particular implications. A crisis could "untie the tongues and break the old constraints."[40]

Although the National Front, a party which holds thirty five seats in the French National Assembly, harbors anti-Semitism as a hidden political agenda, and whose leadership has repeatedly been charged with Jew-hatred, the Jewish issue is not being used overtly as a political weapon in France today. But, from 1967 to 1982, as a result of foreign policy decisions and the erosion of taboos imposed by the Jewish tragedy in World War II, echoes of past attitudes to Jews resurfaced. The pages which follow outline this development, beginning with President De Gaulle's 1967 press conference. Subsequent chapters deal with the effects of De Gaulle's policies, and with the loosening of rhetorical constraints in the media, including one of France's most influential "institutions," the daily, *Le Monde*. The public rediscovery of France's treatment of the Jews during the Vichy period, the positions on Zionism and Jews of the left and of the right, as well as the socio-cultural and religious changes in a revitalized, politically mobilized French-Jewish community, are also examined.

# Notes

[1]P. Higonnet, "On the Extent of Anti-Semitism in Modern France," in F. Malino and B. Wasserstein, eds., *The Jews in Modern France* (Hanover and London: University Press of New England, 1985), p. 207.

[2]Jeffrey Mehlman, *Legacies of Anti-Semitism in France* (Minneapolis: University of Minnesota Press, 1983), p. 4.

[3]L. Dawidowicz, *The Jewish Presence* (New York: Holt, Rinehart and Winston, 1977), p. 213.

[4]*Warrant for Genocide, The Myth of the Jewish World-Conspiracy and the Protocols of the Elders of Zion* (London: Eyre and Spottiswoode, 1967), p. 16, n. 2.

[5]*Réflexions sur la question juive* (Paris: Gallimard, 1954), p. 92.

[6]M. Winock, *Edouard Drumont et Cie, antisémitisme et fascisme en France* (Paris: Seuil, 1982) p. 69.

[7]B.-H. Lévy, *L'Idéologie française* (Paris: Grasset, 1981), p. 123.

[8]See Z. Sternhell, *La Droite révolutionnaire, les origines françaises du Fascisme 1885-1914* (Paris: Seuil, 1978).

[9]D.S. Landes, "Two Cheers for Emancipation," in Malino and Wasserstein, *The Jew in Modern France*, p. 302.

[10]Eugen Weber, in *National Revival in France, 1905-1914* (Berkeley: University of California Press, 1959), pp. 21-23, cited in Landes, *The Jews in Modern France* p. 302.

[11]L. Poliakov, *De Moscou à Beyrouth* (Paris: Calmann-Lévy, 1983), p. 16.

[12]*Ibid.*, pp. 18-19.

[13]Mehlman, *Legacies of Anti-Semitism in France*, p. 61.

[14]Higonnet, *The Jews in Modern France*, p. 210.

[15]Cited in Mehlman, *Legacies of Anti-Semitism in France*, p. 11.

[16]*Réflexions sur la question juive*, p. 92.

[17]R. Aron, *De Gaulle, Israël et les Juifs* (Paris: Plon, 1968), p. 12.

[18]*Ibid.*, p. 17.

[19]*Le Monde*, Oct. 9, 1980.

[20]A. Harris and A. de Sédouy, *Juifs et Français* (Paris: Grasset, 1979), p. 9.

[21]*Pour en finir avec l'antisémitisme* (Paris: Julliard, 1979).

[22]R. Wistrich, "The Anti-Zionist Masquerade," *Midstream*, Vol. XXIX, no. 7 (August-September, 1983), p. 13.

[23]F. Furet, *L'Atelier de l'histoire* (Paris: Flammarion, 1982), p. 299.

[24]E. Le Roy Ladurie, in "Dérapage de la gauche?", *Les Nouveaux cahiers*, no. 71 (Winter, 1982-1983), p. 21.

[25]R. Wistrich, *The Left Against Zion* (London: Vallentine, 1979), p. VII.

26Reported in *The Canadian Jewish News*, Nov. 27, 1986.

27B. Barret-Kriegel, *Les Nouveaux cahiers*, no. 71, p. 10.

28*La Réprobation d'Israël* (Paris: Denoël-Gonthier, 1983), p. 63.

29*Ibid.*, p. 132.

30*L'Atelier de l'histoire*, p. 286.

31Michael R. Marrus has claimed, for instance, that anti-Semitism is not a unique phenomenon and that it may disappear in the next generation ("Are the French Anti-Semitic?", *Jerusalem Quarterly*, no. 32 Summer, 1984, pp. 95-96). For a spirited response to Marrus' unhistorical approach to anti-Semitism, and to his other arguments denying or minimizing contemporary anti-Semitism, presented in his article, "Is There A New Antisemitism?," in *Middle East Focus*, Vol. VI, no. 4 (November, 1983), see Frederick Krantz, *Middle East Focus*, Vol. VII, no. 1 (May, 1984) pp. 20-23. Curiously, Marrus has also suggested that the French neo-Nazis who deny the Holocaust may merely be motivated by a "French attraction to a sharp polemic" (*Jerusalem Quarterly*, no. 32, p. 90).

32N. Cohn, *Warrant for Genocide*, p. 254.

33After citing opinion polls which apparently prove that hostility to Jews in France is low, Michael R. Marrus notes, without explanation, that "just over half the populatiuon believed after the bombing [of the rue Copernic synagogue] that anti-Semitism was fairly widespread...." (*Jerusalem Quarterly*, p. 95).

34*The Jewish Presence*, p. 212.

35P Jarreau, *Information juive* (June, 1985).

36Y. Bauer, "Anti-Semitism Today—A Fact or a Fiction?," *Midstream*, Vol. XXX, n. 8 (October, 1984), p. 30.

37*Ibid*, p. 28.

38*La République et les Juifs* (Paris: Les Presses d'Aujourd'hui, 1982), p. 34.

39Marrus' claim that this bias has been "strongly exaggerated" (*Jerusalem Quarterly*, pp. 88-89), is contradicted by prominent French scholars: A. Finkielkraut, *La Réprobation d'Israël*; A. Kriegel, *Israël est-il coupable?* (Paris: Laffont, 1982); L. Poliakov, *De Moscou à Beyrouth*; B. Barret-Kriegel, E. Le Roy Ladurie, D. Lindenberg and P.-A. Taguieff in *Les Nouveaux cahiers*, no. 71, pp. 9-22.; S. Trigano, "From Individual to Collectivity: The Rebirth of the 'Jewish Nation' in France," in Malino and Wasserstein, *The Jews in Modern France*, pp. 270-271.

40A. Finkielkraut, *Le Juif imaginaire* (Paris: Seuil, 1980), p. 116.

# CHAPTER I

# The General and the Domineering People

Having liquidated the painful war in Algeria President Charles De Gaulle set out to rebuild bridges to a civilization with which France had developed a special relationship over the last two centuries. In renewing ties with the Arab world De Gaulle hoped to exercise geopolitical influence denied to him in other parts of the globe, and at the same time to gain markets for a modernizing and expanding economy. France's dependence on oil supplies and its development of a modern arms industry provided further motivations for a rapprochement with the Arabs. De Gaulle is said to have put it bluntly to one of his most trusted lieutenants: there are a hundred times more Arabs than Jews in the Mediterranean basin. To carry out the policy reorientation De Gaulle needed an opportunity to distance himself from Israel in a manner that could dramatically project him as an ally of the Arab cause, while protecting him from the reaction of pro-Israeli public opinion.

The French President, who had once publically called Israel a "friendly and allied State," was not unaware that he could not exercise his policy change without finding for it a moral justification; the purely political motives of *Realpolitik* were insufficient in a relationship that involved more than commerce and military co-operation. He realized that the outpouring of sympathy and concern for the safety of Israel in the weeks prior to the start of the Six Day War hostilities, and the jubilation in the streets of Paris after Israel's swift victory, indicated that deep emotions were involved and that an annulment of the tacit alliance with Israel, that had existed for more than a decade, would arouse strong protests in both Jewish and non-Jewish circles.

In the post-war period, prior to 1967, anti-Semitism had ceased to be a public issue and the majority of the French admired the courage of the new Israeli state, successfully battling an Arab world that had managed to humiliate France in North Africa. When, in 1954, the philosopher Jean-Paul Sartre, published a perceptive study on anti-Semitism, *Réflexions sur la question juive*, he seemed to refer to a phenomenon from the past, with little relevance to the post-war period. Following the Holocaust, the debates over the place of Jews in French society that had stirred so many passions earlier in the century appeared to have vanished. Even the militant anti-Semites seemed to have decided to submerge their feelings, in deference to the dead or because the enormity of the tragedy had removed the seedbed in which their notions could thrive.

The man who renewed the debate over the "Jewish question" in France was, paradoxically, the leader who led French opposition to Vichy Fascism in World War II. It was General Charles De Gaulle who, five months after the Six Day War, at a press conference, became the first major Western head of state of the post-Holocaust era to link criticism of the State of Israel with references to stereotypic images of the Jew. In a maneuver to reorient French foreign policy toward the oil-rich Arab States, the President of France reinserted racial generalisations into political discourse. For the first time since the creation of the Jewish state a prominent Western leader attempted to justify political decisions, the termination of the alliance, the imposition of an arms embargo on Israel and the completion of an arms deal with one of its enemies, by castigating Israeli policies allegedly dictated by racial character traits.

The implications of the November 27, 1967, press conference went beyond the notorious pronouncement that Jews were an "elite," "domineering" and "self-assured" people.[1] The significance of the remarks was considerably wider: in his lengthy address De Gaulle used anti-Semitic clichés as a justification for his abandonment of close ties with Israel, distorted historical facts, and implied, among other slurs, that the Jewish people was prone to aggression. Some of these ideas echoed the views of one of De Gaulle's mentors, the influential twentieth-century writer and political thinker, Charles Maurras, who was profoundly anti-Semitic.[2] Whether De Gaulle's utterances were a conscious expression of Maurras-inspired anti-Semitism, or notions subconsciously absorbed from his nationalistic philosophy, his phrase characterizing the Jewish people — the people as a whole — as a domineering, self-assured elite, legitimized a renewal of Jew-baiting. The General's remarks also brought about a new rift between French Jews and non-Jews: "old links were broken, old friendships came to an end, suspicions and a new source of divisions reappeared."[3]

De Gaulle's comments seemed to have suddenly removed a protective shield that, since 1945, imposed a taboo on open hostility toward the survivors of Hitler's crimes. Although the General later claimed that his references to the character of the Jewish people were meant as a compliment, they constituted a racial, collective characterization. A French-Jewish thinker commented that the reference to Jewish domination implicitly negated the Holocaust, and projected "exactly the same stereotype of the Jew as might be held by a provincial hardware store owner...the image of Jewish power, of the Jewish desire to dominate,"[4] and that De Gaulle's public pronouncement on the Jewish character revealed that a "common anti-Semitic stereotype had been present in his mind for a long time."[5] Inevitably, De Gaulle's widely quoted statements stirred up a variety of forgotten suspicions. Echoes of the Jewish conspiracy theme and of alleged Jewish domination of certain sectors of the French economy became a topic of discussion.

The shocking affront to Israel and the Jewish people created a dilemma for French Jews, especially those who viewed themselves primarily as Frenchmen. In a country where the traditional Jacobin spirit of the French Revolution dictated an undivided loyalty to the State, even those who considered it their right to maintain links with their ancient people were faced with a challenge that was not easy to confront. Supporting Israel now involved arousing suspicions and risking the loss of acceptance in a society that does not tolerate minorities easily. Standing aside, on the other hand, meant betraying one's profound instincts of solidarity with the survivors of an unprecedented genocide.

In his statement explaining France's new Middle-Eastern policy de Gaulle inermingled his interpretation of Israel's political behavior with historical "explanations" which smacked of anti-Semitism. "Some feared," he said concerning the reborn Jewish state, "that once reunited in the city of their former grandeur they would convert their profound wishes into a burning ambition for conquest." The clear implication was that Israel was indeed an expansionist state, as the Arab propaganda contended. In the course of the press conference De Gaulle also stated or intimated, among other, that: throughout history, Jews have "provoked" anti-Semitism, that they are immensely rich, and that they possess the means to exercise inordinate influence and mount massive propaganda campaigns. De Gaulle implicitly characterized the Israelis as arrogant, expansionist war hawks who seek every opportunity to achieve their imperialistic aims, as militarists spoiling for a fight. He also "invited" the Jews to keep a low profile, implying that Israel's right to live in security was linked to the "humility" of its political behavior.

Anti-Semitism, De Gaulle explained, was due to "waves of antagonism" ("malveillances") that Jews "had provoked, more precisely had aroused in certain countries and at certain times." The Jews, he added, ought to be grateful for the sympathy that was offered to them, "in spite of" recurrent "tides of antagonism" they had "provoked." The implication was that the victim was guilty of instigating the violence against it. After the press conference, a group of intellectuals commented: "these historical considerations about Jews are close to slander and can revive anti-Semitic hatred . . . they justify retroactively centuries of pogroms and millions of slaughtered."[6] The General's assertions did not explain how, through the centuries, this "self-assured people" somehow managed to present an easy target for murderous mobs. De Gaulle also spoke of the relations between the Jews and the Church and declared that Christendom held a "considerable capital...of sympathy" toward Jews, ignoring such facts that even in modern times the Church was among the leading forces behind anti-Jewish witch hunts like the anti-Dreyfus campaign, or that in Medieval France the Crusaders instigated some of the first pogroms on record in Europe.

The French president also observed that his country had "consented" to the establishment of the State of Israel, in spite of the fact that it received "vast assistence in money, influence, and propaganda from Jewish circles ("mileux") in America, Europe and many other countries, including France." This assertion mimicked a popular anti-Semitic myth: Jews are rich, and use their money to exercise improper influence through the media which they own. The words "influence and propaganda" echoed the myth of Jewish control of the press, and the terms "vast," "money," "influence" alleged pernicious manipulation of the world of finance. The word "milieu," which in French can also refer to the underworld, carried with it negative connotations of the illicit and the unsavory. The fact that these clichés were pronounced from the majestic forum of the Elysée Palace, by the most imposing French political figure of the twentieth century, added gravity to the allegations.

The French President also charged that, already in the 1956 "Sinai Campaign," Israel appeared "as a war-like State determined to expand." He did not accept the more objective explanation, that the 1956 incursion into the Sinai peninsula was an attempt to liquidate terrorist bases, while taking advantage of the Franco-British expedition to regain control over the Suez Canal. De Gaulle also found Israel guilty of what he referred to as "internal expansionism." The Jewish State, he charged, "acted *to double*" its population (in fact it tried to cope with a million refugees from transit camps in Germany and from Arab lands), and "aroused the suspicion" that the "territory it acquired would not meet its needs for very long and it would be *inclined to increase it, using every opportunity* that presented itself to do so."[7] The reference to acquisition, expansion, and opportunism reflected other stereotypic images prevalent in French popular lore and fiction: those of the grabbing, unscrupulous and opportunistic Jew.

Throughout the press conference the interchangeable use of the terms "the Jewish people" and "Israel," implied that the alleged negative "character traits" of the one, and the political behavior of the other, stemmed from a common defective hereditary source. This link was reinforced by the fact that the French term "Israélite" (Jew), is barely distinguishable from the newer term "Israélien" (Israeli). De Gaulle suggested that Israeli "expansionism" and "aggression" were bred into the Jewish character and constituted traditional Jewish traits. He also indirectly reiterated the allegation of Jewish arrogance ("self-assurance" in the notorious phrase), by asking Israel to treat its neighbors with "greater modesty."

In the General's view, even the Six Day War stemmed from Israeli opportunism and aggressiveness: "The Akaba affair [the Egyptian blockade of the Gulf of Akaba, in May 1967] offered a pretext to those eager to cross swords ... in six days of fighting Israel *grabbed the objectives it wished to attain*."[8] The message was that the Israelis, eager for a war, were merely waiting for the opportunity to seize Arab lands. Somehow, the sudden mobilization of an army comprised almost entirely of reservists, the foreboding atmosphere that reigned in Israel in the weeks prior to the outbreak of hostilities, the mass slaughter promised by gleeful announcers on Radio Cairo, eluded the General's analysis.

The cumulative portrait of the Jewish people drawn by De Gaulle corresponded to a compendium of the crudest anti-Semitic stereotypes: Jews are domineering, arrogant, opportunistic, aggressive, immensely rich, and use their great wealth and influence to manipulate the media. To compound the offense, in using these smears as a justification for changes in his Middle Eastern policy the French President reintroduced anti-Semitism as a political tool, thus reverting to a darker period in his country's history. It was obvious that he greatly harmed the post-Holocaust efforts to eradicate anti-Semitism. Moreover, De Gaulle not only revived and awarded respectability to old apocryphal charges, but also transferred them to the new Jewish State.

The reactions in the French and Israeli press, as well as the statements issued by Jewish and non-Jewish French leaders, indicated that not everyone accepted De Gaulle's denials of anti-Semitic motivation. Some of his closest former associates noted that he was a man who could display "remarkable bad faith."[9] *Le Monde*, not usually known for its sensitivity on Jewish issues, detected "anti-Semitic scents."[10] Jean Lecanuet, the President of the Democratic Centre Party, was "deeply shocked . . . and discerned anti-Semitism in certain phrases."[11] The Socialist leader, Guy Mollet, found in De Gaulle's words "a pseudo-historical explanation of the Jewish character that is both unjust and insulting."[12] The mayor of Marseilles, Gaston Defferre, also noted anti-Jewish connotations: "for De Gaulle there is a difference between Jews and those who practice other religions. This is the real significance of the matter . . . it can serve as a basis for anti-Semitism."[13]

Xavier Vallat, the former Vichy Commissioner for Jewish Affairs, wrote gleefully in the right-wing weekly, *Aspects de la France*, that until De Gaulle's anti-Jewish pronouncements, journalists who dared to say that "the Jewish people...is imbued with its superiority and considers itself destined . . . to dominate the world," were immediately hauled into a court of justice.[14] Illustrating the impact of De Gaulle's anti-Semitic lesson, a youth organization, "The Union of Youth for Progress," issued a statement that "it approved the totality of General De Gaulle's remarks."

In Israel, the left-wing daily, *Al Hamishmar*, judged the De Gaulle's remarks to be "full of hatred toward Israel, Zionism and Judaism" and accused the French President of professing pure anti-Semitism. Another newspaper, *Hayom*, pointed to the *Protocols of the Elders of Zion* as De Gaulle's inspiration, and the Israeli poet, Chaim Gouri, qualified the tirade as a "primitive anti-Semitic sermon" and urged the government to recall its Ambassador from

Paris. In the Arab world a jubilant press proclaimed De Gaulle "the first leader...to denounce Israel's expansionist policy."[15]

The reaction inside the French Jewish community was characterized by the subdued anger of the Chief Rabbi, Jacob Kaplan, who asked if "by imputing that the Jewish people is inclined toward secular domination...General de Gaulle did not take the risk of opening a dangerous path, and of giving the highest possible sanction to a campaign of discrimination."[16] The French-Jewish press responded with a mixture of shock and bewilderment to the fact that a leader in the fight against Nazi Germany could utter racial remarks. One Jewish weekly wrote that it was "filled with sadness and stupefied by cruel reminiscences and tragic associations."[17] Even the anti-Zionist historian, Pierre Vidal-Naquet, denounced the "anti-Semitic scent."[18]

Soon, however, eager to be reassured, some of De Gaulle's Jewish critics declared that they were satisfied with his explanations. Only six weeks after the press conference the Chief Rabbi stated, following a meeting with De Gaulle, that his fears had been allayed and that "the General's remarks about Jews are now a closed chapter." "Grand Rabbin" Kaplan also added: "we were really afraid about the possibility of an outbreak of a new wave of anti-Semitism in France, but after my conversation with General de Gaulle my apprehension has disappeared."[19] The Jewish Gaullist politician, Claude-Gérard Marcus, concurred: "the General's explanation dispels all anxiety."[20] It was obvious that the hope that the affair would soon be forgotten, and a desire to blot out painful memories, prompted the quick acceptance of De Gaulle's reassurances.

Paradoxically, some non-Jews did not accept the General's version of the meaning of his statements, and did not hesitate to label him in unequivocal terms as an anti-Semite. Thus, revealing testimony concerning the General's feelings about Jews came from a prominent political figure, the former Foreign Minister, Christian Pineau. Although he did not attribute the 1967 policy change entirely to prejudice, Pineau stated that De Gaulle "was profoundly anti-Semitic," that this fact was "not sufficiently known," and that he had "always known De Gaulle to be an anti-Semite and an ardent disciple of Charles Maurras."[21]

Jewish and pro-Israeli Gaullists were torn between loyalty to their leader and devotion to truth and principles. Before the outbreak of the Six Day War, when France declared its neutrality and imposed an embargo on arms shipments to the Middle East, a

Gaullist member of parliament complained about a "betrayal of the most cherished principles."[22] Others expressed shock and outrage over the embargo which hurt Israel far more than it did the Arabs. But when De Gaulle, in an attempt to stifle criticism of his policies, demanded action against parliamentarians from his party who intended to participate in a pro-Israel rally, many submitted to the pressure. Some, like Léo Hamon, a prominent Jewish Gaullist, "escaped into total silence."[23] Most pro-Israeli Gaullists, even the founders of the "France-Israel Association," did not react, even though "it was a question of violating a commitment by France."[24]

The birth of the State of Israel has added a new dimension to the existence of Diaspora Jewry. Pride, concern and solidarity have shaped the attitude of Jews in dispersion to their revived ancestral homeland. Whereas in the United States, Canada and to a similar degree in Great Britain, the devotion of the Jews to Israel has generally met with approval and even admiration on the part of the non-Jewish population, in France, following General De Gaulle's 1967 shift in Middle Eastern policy, the Jewish community has had to contend with repeated accusations of double loyalty. When they attempted to seek a change in the government's hostile policies toward the Jewish state French Jews found out that their country was still too monolithic to tolerate sympathy for another state. Even feeble protests against clearly pro-Arab attitudes and political measures met with hostility in government circles, and with a lack of sympathy in the media, which in France, often back the foreign policy of the government in power.

A year after De Gaulle's press conference, a writer who identified himself as a Gaullist wrote: "Israel is a pure colonial fact, the metropolis of an omnipresent and imperceptible empire that uses the Old Testament for less than religious purposes."[25] The terms "omnipresent" and "imperceptible empire" conjured up the old image of world domination by invisible, slippery and cleverly deceptive conspirators. The word "metropolis" played on the negative image of Jewish cosmopolitanism and alluded to Jerusalem as the seat of an evil conspiracy. The giant octopus (this "metropolis") that reaches out to every corner of the world was a reference to one of the themes echoed in the *Protocols of the Elders of Zion*.[26]

Irked by public support for Israel in the wake of the Six Day War other Gaullists picked up on the refrain of alleged domination by Jews of the press and radio.[27] A former Government minister stated that Jews "have in their hands many of the means of social communication."[28] A member of the cabinet spoke of Israeli "influences" in "circles close to the media."[29] According to one of De Gaulle's closest confidants, the former Minister Alain Peyrefitte, the General himself believed that Jews were too prominent in the French media.[30] A senior Gaullist party official deplored "the powerful" offensive "unleashed" against the General's Middle East policy. It is ironic that the myth of Jewish control of the media should have been revived in France, where Jewish journalists tend to have leftist views and often voice harsh criticism of Israel. It was even more ironic that these journalists, who often bend over backwards to prove their objectivity on issues pertaining to Jews or to Israel, should have been portrayed as agents of a mighty Jewish establishment.

The historical significance of De Gaulle's November, 1967 pronouncements and the potential harm to world Jewry they contained, was outlined in a book entitled *De Gaulle, Israel and the Jews*, by the distinguished scholar and publicist, Raymond Aron. Prophetically, Aron wrote, the General's press conference "solemnly *authorised*" a new anti-Semitism.[31] Referring to the charge of domination and elitism, and to Christianity's alleged sympathy for Jews, Aron commented, sarcastically: "this piece of literary bravado would elicit only a shrug if the orator did not take the entire world as witness to his genius."[32] For De Gaulle, he noted, "had knowingly, voluntarily, opened a new era in Jewish history and perhaps in the history of anti-Semitism."[33] All of a sudden state anti-Semitism became again "salonfähig," since Jew-haters received permission from the head of state "to use the same language as before the great massacre."[34]

Aron also deplored the silence of prominent French intellectuals on the affair. In the preface to his book, he revealed that he was reluctantly forced to respond to the General's tirade because such famous voices as those of the writers, François Mauriac and André Malraux, intimates of De Gaulle, remained silent. Alas, he noted, "none of these writers, representing the honor of French letters, none of those who so many times speak in the name of universal conscience,"[35] reacted to De Gaulle's anti-Semitic outburst. As time was to prove, this first notable silence of the highly influential intellectual world that normally responds to less serious infringements on the dignity of man, in France and elsewhere in the world, was to set a pattern that was in itself a measure of a double standard toward the Jewish community.

Then, as later, "so many who ought to have heard [the injustice] didn't."[36]

In 1980, a French-Jewish writer recalled De Gaulle's 1967 press conference and reflected on the meaning of his words: "My instinctive reaction was correct, I realized that the General's declaration was an expression of traditional anti-Semitism ... it represented a prejudice deeply rooted in the mentality of the French bourgeoisie. Thirteen years later I have not changed my mind."[37] Another prominent figure in the French Jewish community remarked on the impact of the General's speech on events that followed: "De Gaulle opened the path to official tolerance of the most extreme Arab views and of suspicions against Jews which fed and legitimized anti-Semitism ... His successors have been most faithful to this path."[38]

Before he set out to write his book Raymond Aron was, according to his own testimony, urged not to respond to De Gaulle's comments. The timid advised him that it was best to remain silent on this "poisoned theme" because one risked irritating non-Jews as well as Jews. Many in the Jewish community, either because they considered themselves totally assimilated into French society, and therefore immune, or because of fear, or resignation to the existence of anti-Semitism, preferred not to react. Some, displaying an attitude reminiscent of the "Jewish Frenchmen" in the 1930s, who disassociated themselves from the Eastern European Jewish immigrants, went as far as to declare that the General's remarks were only directed at the Israelis, that they did not concern "truly French Jews" like themselves.

One of the "patriotic" French Jews published an article in Le Monde which attacked De Gaulle's Jewish critics. The author of the article expressed shock that Jews would dare to criticize the President of the French Republic. Jewish criticism "betrayed a sentiment that could be associated with a kind of double loyalty."[39] The Le Monde contributor wondered how anyone, "claiming to belong to the 'chosen people'," could be upset by the term "domination." The "Jewish Frenchman" went on to explain that De Gaulle's comments were not directed at patriotic French Jews but only against "the Jewish people throughout its migrations and the State of Israel." The French Jews, he commented, who demonstrated support for Israel during the Six Day War, who "took sides," were guilty of "indecency." He added a remark worthy of anti-Semites: "as soon as one speaks about them, Jews generally see in this malice, perfidy, malevolence."

A few months earlier, *Le Monde*, which carefully selects the few letters to the editor it prints, published a long letter by another Jewish reader who objected to Baron Edmond de Rothschild's call for financial assistance to Israel following the Six Day War, in opposition to De Gaulle's apparent wishes. The letter claimed that the Baron's appeal for funds was "only supplying a weapon to anti-Semitism." It further stated that those who are loyal to the Jewish people, "who consider themselves as belonging to the 'chosen people', are just as racist as the anti-Semites."[40] In the 1960s, Jewish self-hatred was apparently not a rare phenomenon in France. The homogenizing pressures of French society seemed to produce an inordinate craving to belong to the majority culture, to acquire the right to true "francité" (Frenchness).

If the main motivation for De Gaulle's November, 1967, address was the need to find a pretext for the reorientation of his Middle Eastern policy, he also let it be known that he was personally offended by the outpouring of pro-Israeli sentiment during the Six Day War. He reportedly took umbrage at what he viewed as, open "collusion" with a foreign state. The General was "painfuly surprised" by the "attitude of most French Jews," wrote a prominent columnist, he was shocked that men close to his government "could adopt a stance against government policy, for Israel and against France...That was simply inconceivable, unacceptable!"[41] The specter of dual allegiance was brandished by the highest authority of the state. There were persistent reports that Jews were fired from posts in the government-controlled radio and television.

The security of the French state could not have been threatened by the pro-Israeli street demonstrations, which represented, after all, a natural human reaction on the part of French Jewry toward the plight of the Israelis, many of them Holocaust survivors. The concern for Israel's survival in the weeks prior to the outbreak of the Six Day War was so intense, that it affected even marginal Jews. Only the callous could remain indifferent. Understandably, even former anti-Zionists, agnostics and the completely assimilated felt pangs of anguish over the possibility of another Holocaust. A well-known novelist, brought up as a Christian and barely remembering her Jewish origins, later recalled how "she trembled with deep concern" for the fate of the Jewish state in the spring of 1967.[42] The implication that such a natural human reaction could be considered treasonous aroused bewilderment. "How much sympathy [for Israel] can we be permitted without being accused of double loyalty?" asked Raymond Aron.[43]

A ringing answer to Aron's question came in the form of a *Le Monde* article entitled "Double Allegiance."[44] A former senior member of the French Foreign Ministry, René Massigli, stated that "the tradition of our Revolution does not permit double allegiance." He claimed that since the creation of the State of Israel, in 1948, there has been a "latent risk" of a "split in the block of French unity." His designation of French Jewry as an element potentially harmful to the national interest was accompanied by direct threats of retribution. French Jews, wrote the senior diplomat, "risk facing one day the choice of accepting either French or Israeli citizenship." He added, ominiously: "may this folly never be committed...."

The Massigli article also echoed a well-worn anti-Semitic charge: Jews are an inimical, foreign body in societies in which they live. Recalling the bloodshed that was caused by religious wars in French history he issued a warning: "It is well known what price had to be paid ... what civil strife ... May our compatriots who identify with the cause of Israel refrain from inciting us to apply similar means adapted from the past. The consequences could be disastrous to them...." It was significant that the most influential French daily printed this undisguised attempt to blackmail a group of law-abiding citizens. Responding to the article, the novelist Romain Gary, who seldom identified himself as a Jew, wrote that "the imaginary perils" mentioned in the *Le Monde* article "represent an attempt to intimidate, if not anti-Semitic blackmail."[45] Leaders of the Jewish community, however, failed to focus public attention on the scandalous and defamatory article, containing threats and bordering on incitement to racial violence. They did not alert public opinion to the fact that collective accusations of treason are not simply innocent viewpoints.

# Notes

[1]*Le Monde*, Nov. 29, 1967.

[2]P. Serant, *Les Dissidents de l'Action Française* (Paris: Editions Copernic, 1978), p. 310. On Maurras' influence on twentieth-century French ideology see

Chapter VI.

[3]Pierre Viansson-Ponté, "Le Général et le peuple Juif," *Le Monde*, Dec. 13, 1967.

[4]Arnold Mandel, *Nous autres Juifs* (Paris: Hachette, 1978), p. 61.

[5]*Ibid.*, p. 63.

[6]*Le Monde*, Dec. 2, 1967. The signatories of the statement included such well-known thinkers and writers as Vladimir Jankélévitch, Jean-Pierre Faye and Jean-François Revel.

[7]Emphasis added.

[8]Emphasis added.

[9]E. Pisani quoted in P. Wajsman and R.-F. Teissèdre, *Nos politiciens face au conflit israélo-arabe* (Paris: Fayard, 1969), p. 143.

[10]*Le Monde*, Nov. 29, 1967.

[11]*Ibid.*, Dec. 1, 1967.

[12]*Ibid.*, Dec. 2, 1967.

[13]*Ibid.*, Jan. 9, 1968.

[14]Quoted in *Le Monde*, Dec. 10-11, 1967.

[15]*Al Destour* (Amman) quoted in *Le Monde*, Dec. 3-4, 1967.

[16]*Le Monde*, Dec. 1, 1967.

[17]*Le Bulletin de nos communautés*, cited in *Le Monde*, Dec. 1, 1967.

[18]*Le Monde*, Dec. 2, 1967.

[19]*Ibid.*, Jan. 9, 1968.

[20]*Ibid.*, Jan 12, 1968.

[21]Wajsman and Teissèdre, *Nos politiciens*, p. 140.

[22]A. Chalandon, *Le Monde*, June 5, 1967. Cited in S. Cohen, *De Gaulle, les Gaullistes et Israël* (Paris: A. Moreau, 1974), p. 223.

[23]Cohen, *De Gaulle*, p. 230.

[24]Wajsman and Teissèdre, *Nos politiciens*, p. 144.

[25]P. de Saint-Robert, "Terrorisme ou résistance?," *Le Monde*, Feb. 7, 1969.

[26]The myth alleging a Jewish scheme to conquer the world, conceived in nineteenth-century France and disseminated by the Tzar's Ochrana, was fanned by Hitler's propaganda machine. More recently it has been reprinted in Arab States, and Soviet information services have borrowed concepts from it.

[27]André Philip in *La Réforme*, 1967. Cited in Léon Poliakov, *De l'antisionisme à l'antisémitisme* (Paris: Calmann-Lévy, 1969), p. 158.

[28]Edmond Michelet, cited in Cohen, *De Gaulle*, p. 209.

[29]Joël Le Theule, cited in Cohen, *De Gaulle*, p. 209.

[30]Peyrefitte revealed this fact in a conversation with this writer in Paris, in May, 1982.

[31]*De Gaulle, Israël et les Juifs*, p. 12.

[32]*Ibid.*, p. 16.

[33]*Ibid.*, p. 18.

[34]*Ibid.*, p. 17.

[35]*Ibid.*, p. 7.

[36]*Ibid.*, p. 13.

[37]A. Mandel, *Le Journal de nos communautés*, December, 1980.

[38]Emile Touati, *Le Journal de nos communautés*, December, 1980.

[39]Roger Stéphane, "Juifs français et Français juifs," *Le Monde*, Dec. 6, 1967.

[40]J. Hamadard, *Le Monde*, July 9-10, 1967.

[41]Viansson-Ponté, *Le Monde*, Dec. 13, 1967.
[42]Natalie Sarraute in a conversation with this writer.
[43]*De Gaulle, Israël et les Juifs*, p. 42.
[44]Feb. 27, 1970.
[45]"Disqualification raciale," *Le Monde*, March 1-2, 1970.

# CHAPTER II

# Embargoes and Suspect Loyalties

A year after his press conference, using as a pretext an Israeli retaliatory raid on Beirut airport, De Gaulle imposed a total embargo on military equipment to Israel, including fifty fighter-planes Israel had ordered two years earlier and had already paid for. The decision to deprive the Jewish state of vital means of defense seemed both harsh and unjustified. Some editorialists questioned the general's motives and suggested that they may have been other than political. The action, wrote a commentator in *Combat*, "is a new manifestation of this anti-Semitism inspired by Maurras."[1] De Gaulle "was a faithful executor of the thought of Charles Maurras,"[2] wrote another Paris newspaper.

Ignoring the repeated acts of terrorism that prompted the Israeli reprisal, the French government condemned the allegedly "excessive" use of force against a country with "traditional" ties of friendship to France. The fact that the Israeli raiders painstak-ingly avoided inflicting human casualties and destroyed only empty airplanes parked on runways, which terrorists had used freely to travel to their destinations of crime, did not provide mitigating circumstances in the eyes of the French officials. "Why this silence over the terrorist attack in Athens [against an EL AL airliner] and in a Jerusalem market (where many civilians had been killed and injured), and so many protests over the raid in Beirut?," a Paris columnist asked.[3] It became apparent from offi-cial statements and commentaires on the state-run radio and television, that the government was building up a case against Israel in order to justify its new embargo. Since France was the almost exclusive supplier of military equipment to the Jewish state, the embargo was a highly discriminatory measure that had to be justified in front of a public opinion that continued to be sympathetic toward Israel.

While the government inflated the gravity of Israeli measures against terrorists for political reasons, the condemnations of Israel spilled over into accusations of dual loyalty against French Jewry. Not only were large arms sales to the Arabs "proper," because of Israeli "excesses," official sources argued, they also represented a show of independence from "powerful" pressures of the "Jewish lobby" in France. Unable, or unwilling to understand the deep emotional attachement to Israel among Jews, the authorities reacted to Jewish protests against their policies in the Middle East by brandishing the specter of Jewish "domination" over the media. If, previously, such charges were heard from lower-level functionaires and ardent supporters of De Gaulle, they now came from the top, the Prime Minister's office. Its spokesman, Joël Le Theule, declared: "it has been noted that Israeli influences have made themselves felt in circles close to the media."[4] A *Combat* editorialist responded sarcastically that "no doubt" all French journalists were on "Israel's payroll."

De Gaulle's government used other occasions to condemn Israel and to silence criticism of its own decisions. Thus, earlier, in March 1968, an arms deals with Iraq coincided with the demand by the French representative at the United Nations, Armand Bérard, that Israel be condemned for a reprisal raid into Jordan. Protests by French Jews provoked tirades questioning their loyalty to France. Answering questions of listeners on a radio programme dealing with the arms embargo, the Prime Minister, Michel Debré, let it be known that the government would not tolerate "pressures" that are not "in the interest of France."[5] There are definite limits to criticism, he stated, and hinted that those who transgressed them should expect to be brought to account. Referring to his spokesman's denunciation of "Israeli influences" in the media a listener remarked to the Prime Minister: "I can't help noticing in it a scent of anti-Semitism and echoes of the expression, 'sold to the Jews', which we had forgotten in our country . . . ." Debré responded that "among Frenchmen . . . , there is only one thing that matters, and that is the problem of France . . . any influence that is not in the general interest may one day be denounced."[6] The message was veiled, but unmistakable, and it came from the second-highest political figure in the country: unless the critics of the Gaullist Middle Eastern policy kept silent, they risked accusations of disloyalty and undefined consequences.

Other defenders of the government's stance voiced even more blunt threatening and defamatory statements. In March, 1969, *Le*

*Monde* published an article by a Gaullist politician who amplified on De Gaulle's by now familiar pronouncements: "of course Jews behave as a 'self-assured and domineering' people as soon as they feel in a position of strength. They exasperate their best friends and try the patience of angels." The article also referred to "Jewish Nazis" and to the Holocaust: "there are many of us who are fed up with the blackmail about Hitler's persecutions."[7] Another well-known Gaullist charged that Israel "tries to use Jewish organizations, to put pressure on all Jews in all countries" to further its aims, without regard to "consequences."[8] The nature of the "consequences" was not spelled out.

The Gaullist anger disguised a heavy dose of cynicism which was intended to cover up the rapidly expanding arms sales to the Arab states. In 1968, the Arabs rewarded De Gaulle with huge orders for French military aircraft, tanks and armoured vehicles. In 1969, Iraq spent $150 million for Mirage V jet fighters and AMX-30 tanks, while Saudi Arabia placed an order for tanks and armoured cars worth $300 million. France got around its embargo on the Middle East by claiming that it applied only to "battlefield" countries: Israel, Egypt, Syria, and Jordan. Thus Iraq, which was a participant in several Arab-Israeli wars since 1948, and refused to sign cease-fire agreements, was considered a non-belligerent state and was allowed to purchase offensive weapons. At the same time, in a secret deal in 1968 Egypt was permitted to buy 500 half-tracks, apparently not considered as offensive weapons.[9] The secret sale, in December 1969, of 102 Mirage jets to Libya, aroused outcries of duplicity and cynicism even in newspapers generally supportive of the government. To no one's surprise, the Libyan Mirages were flown by Egyptian pilots in the 1973 Yom Kippur War.

The government's hostility to Israel was not echoed only in the state-run media. It spread also to independent and religiously-oriented journals. Israeli "vengefulness" soon inspired articles in Catholic publications which compared the "exaggerated" Israeli counter-terrorist measures to acts of vengeance by the Biblical Israelites.[10] One member of the clergy, disturbed by the potential danger of such inflammatory comparisons, asked: "has one thought of the anti-Semitism that can be created when one attempts to compare the nature of the State of Israel with such Biblical examples [of vengeance]?"[11] It was becoming evident that the French government's justifications for its new anti-Israeli policy were creating the potential for new anti-Jewish sentiment.

Following De Gaulle's resignation from office in April, 1969, as a result of a defeat in a referendum, some Gaullists blamed the outcome on the "Jewish vote." Jews were accused of block-voting in an attempt to punish the General for the 1967 Middle East policy switch. One Gaullist charged that "those who camped in France...but feel...that they belong to an 'elite, self-assured and domineering people', have used the role against the General unpatriotically." The indignant Gaullist added that "one day these people will have to chose once and for all, without ambiguity, if they wish to live in France as Frenchmen or live abroad."[12] The referendum was heavily influenced by "Jewish gold," claimed the French representative to the United Nations, Armand Bérard, who spoke of "huge sums of money" coming from pro-Israeli "circles."[13] The novelist, François Mauriac, implied that the referendum defeat was orchestrated by men "not devoid of financial means" who were "infuriated" by De Gaulle's Middle Eastern policy.[14]

In reality, the politically and socially divided, and still relatively small, Jewish community of the 1960s was not a significant electoral factor. Moreover, the community leaders repeatedly expressed their opposition to the mobilization of Jewish votes for any one candidate or issue. Thus, the perception that the Jews had used the ballot to punish De Gaulle was based more on prejudicial convictions than on fact. Yet a senior diplomat echoed the charges of embittered Gaullists about Jewish political homogeneity: "the majority of French Jews never ceased to criticize, to combat and to undermine the Gaullist regime...their opposition influenced the results to the point where it would not be exaggerated to hold them in large part responsible for the outcome."[15]

The unfounded nature of these accusations was underlined by the fact that the difference between the "yes" and the "no" referendum ballot was more than 1,100,000 votes, whereas the total number of Jewish votes was less than 200,000. Even if all Jewish ballots had been cast against De Gaulle their weight could not have been decisive. Yet, the accusations were creating a modern version of an old myth: France is being manipulated by a mighty foreign power, Israel, through the presence on its soil of a "foreign" element, taking its directives from a centre coordinating world-wide activities in Jerusalem.

In December, 1969, France was stirred up by the so-called "Cherbourg Gunboat Affair." Five embargoed gunboats — of twelve purchased by Israel several years earlier — slipped out of the port of Cherbourg with the cooperation of local officials. Some in the press echoed outcries from government sources about "Jewish deception," French "humiliation" and about "complicities" Israel benefited from in France. Allegedly, the Israelis used conspiratorial methods to outwit a "naive" French government, "helpless" in its own country against manipulations by powerful "foreign agents." The Israelis dared to deceive the French government, wrote a prominent journalist, because they have in France "pressure means" and because the Israeli government is "one of the most skilful on the planet."[16] Some Gaullists called for a strong reaction against this "attempt at the prestige and interests" of France.[17] Although the Israelis, who had just lost one of their three submarines to Egyptian torpedo boats considered the need for the French gunboats as vital, a former French Foreign Minister wrote a few years later that the Israelis "had deliberately ridiculed the French authorities."[18]

Predictably, the commotion about the Cherbourg "insult" was soon used as a justification for a further expansion of arms sales to the Arabs. The protests of Israel's sympathizers over the continued embargo on all military equipment to the Jewish state were now rejected with defiance. When questioned at a press conference about the prospect of lifting the embargo on the 50 Mirage jets purchased by Israel, President Georges Pompidou, De Gaulle's successor, replied scornfully: "the number you are calling does not answer." Moreover, he characterized the protests over the discriminatory policy as "delirious." He also denounced Israeli "interference" in French political affairs, Jewish lobbying, and exclaimed angrily: "Abba Eban is not the Foreign Minister of France and Golda Meir is not its Prime Minister. This propaganda [on behalf of Israel] as well as its excesses, which are already noticed by public opinion, must be unmasked."[19] The terms "propaganda," "unmasked," "excesses," carried familiar overtones and repeated an old refrain: Jewish manipulation of public opinion is intolerable and goes against the interests of the state. A journalist who had known him well, revealed that Georges Pompidou had strong feelings of antipathy toward the Israelis and had on several occasions referred to the Ambassador of Israel in Paris, Asher Ben Natan, as the "perfect prototype of a Nazi officer."[20] According to the same source, Pompidou believed that "the right cause was the Arab cause."[21]

Pompidou's trip to the United States in February, 1970, was the occasion of an incident that took on overtones of a confrontation.

Angered by the duplicity of France's behavior in the secret sale of 102 Mirage aircraft to Libya — that had been revealed by the *New York Times* before its confirmation by the French government—[22] American Jews staged demonstrations of protest. In Chicago, as he was leaving the Palmer House Hotel, Jewish demonstrators, some shouting insults, came face-to-face with the French President. Indignant, Pompidou expressed his displeasure in terms that appeared as an attempt to drive a wedge between the "rude" American Jews and their non-Jewish compatriots.

While still on American soil the French President depicted the encounter at the Palmer House as an unlawful, provocative act: "these were carefully organized demonstrations," they "put a blemish on America's forehead." He added: "I send my regards to the population of Chicago, whose great majority, I'm convinced, is ashamed of all this."[23] This attempt to create a split between American Jews and their fellow citizens by a foreign dignitary was unprecedented. Implicit in Pompidou's statement was the suggestion that non-Jewish Chicagoans castigate their Jewish neighbors for their discourtesy to him. In France, the Chicago "affair" was portrayed by the media as a major affront to the French nation and prompted threats against the French Jewish community.[24]

Earlier, in May 1967, Pompidou, then serving as Prime Minister under De Gaulle, spoke of the Jewish presence in the Holy Land as a "foreign body artificially imposed" by Western powers on the Arabs. In the same interview, he compared Israel to a colony like Hong Kong, a western "bridgehead" in the Near East: "In today's strategy, the era of bridgeheads has ended. It would be a disservice to Israel to encourage it to present itself as a bridgehead of the West in the Middle East, like a foreign body artificially imposed by the West on the region."[25] During his trip to the United States, in 1970, Pompidou again referred to Israel as a Western bridgehead in the Middle East. Such statements, a French-Jewish student group declared, "tend to present Jews as agents of a foreign power and provoke a rebirth of anti-Semitism."[26]

American Jews also reacted sharply. They published a full-page advertisement in *The New York Times* accusing Pompidou of "using Arab fanaticism against Israel in order to fill the pockets" of France.[27] To compare the reborn Jewish state to an outpost of Western colonialism, in a region imbued with a millenial physical and spiritual Jewish presence, amounted to a distortion of history. The word "bridgehead" also carried with it echoes of deeply implanted stereotypes. French anti-Semitic lore has often depicted

Jews as intruders, as the "eternal foreigners," in other words, as a fifth column.

President Pompidou also urged Israel to cease being "a racial and religious state" in order to integrate itself into the Middle East.[28] This implication, that the Jewish state espouses a racialist philosophy, represented the first time that a Western leader linked the State of Israel to racism prior to the notorious, 1975 United Nations resolution that equated Zionism with racism. Yet for Maurice Schumann, the Foreign Minister, Pompidou's reference to a racial and religious state was merely a "repudiation of the Zionist temptation." Some suggested that Pompidou's hostility to Israel was even more intense than De Gaulle's.[29] His visit to the United States was followed by a "flood of virulent anti-Jewish publications and anti-Jewish demonstrations at French university campuses."[30] According to a student of Franco-Israeli relations these anti-Jewish outbursts were partly inspired by Pompidou's demands that French Jews choose "between loyalty to France and support for Israel."[31]

Pompidou's declarations aroused alarm and indignation among French Jews. A group of Jewish Resistance fighters pointed out that "this form of anti-Semitism...provokes deep concern among the Jewish population."[32] The President of the League Against Racism, Jean Pierre-Bloch, concluded that branding Israel as a "bridgehead of Western civilization in the Middle East and calling it a racist and religious state invites and justifies aggression." He added, "our head of state may be a non-anti-Semite, but . . . ."[33] An organization of war veterans complained that "anti-Semitic graffiti are multiplying on the walls of Paris, racist propaganda is flourishing in the right-wing press...the failure to prosecute the guilty...can create a propitious climate for all kinds of racists who are spreading hatred against the Jews."[34] Protests from Jews drew, in turn, more accusations of dual loyalty. Foreign Minister Schumann declared that "it was not acceptable for one segment of national opinion to show unconditional fidelity to another nation."[35] There were reports that a high official suggested that Jews serving in posts "essential to national security" be removed.[36]

During Pompidou's tenure as President France's pro-Arab posture intensified. While projecting the image of a potential mediator in the Arab-Israeli conflict, France cast several significant pro-Arab votes at the United Nations, hampered Israel's quest for trading arrangements with the European Economic Community, and backed Soviet proposals for "peace" which were opposed by the United States and Great Britain. France even attempted to sway African delegations to the United Nations to back a Soviet motion on the Middle East.[37] Deputy Minister of Foreign Affairs Jean de Lipkowski, announced in Saudi Arabia that "France believes in the righteousness of the Arabs' position and will continue to lend them its support."[38] The French continued to press Israel to withdraw from occupied territories without demanding from her enemies a declaration of its right to exist. This cynicism was apparently based on the belief that France "had little choice but to assume a pro-Arab stance in light of [the] modest means" at her disposal.[39]

The French government's attitude toward Israel did not undergo change after the Yom Kippur War, even though this time, unlike 1967, it could not be branded as the aggressor. On October 8, 1973, as Israel and the Jewish world were still in shock following the surprise attack by Egypt and Syria, on the holiest of days in the Jewish calendar, the French Foreign Minister, Michel Jobert, made a statement that in the eyes of Israel's sympathizers was marked by callousness. The massive, coordinated sneak attack drew Jobert's laconic comment: "Does an attempt to step back into one's house constitute a surprise aggressive act?" Jobert's "little phrase," as his comment became known, brought an angry reaction from several public figures.[40] Jean Lecanuet, remarked: "Your injustice, Mr. Minister, is obvious to everyone."[41] The French President of the League of Human Rights, Daniel Mayer, commented: "Mr. Jobert's words have less in common with diplomacy than with caddishness."[42] In Paris, Jewish demonstrators shouted, "Jobert, murderer." Shortly after the hostilities Jobert flew to Syria, Egypt, Iraq and Libya to sign new contracts and to assure a steady supply of oil. In Damascus, the French Foreign Minister praised the Arabs' "necessary intransigence." France was exempted from the 1973 Arab oil embargo while on French television the oil crisis was presented in a manner implying Israel's responsibility for it. The process of political separation from Israel begun in 1967 was now complete.

In his electoral campaign promises Valéry Giscard d'Estaing vowed to bring "confidence and clarity" and a new atmosphere to France's relations with the Jewish state. The election of Pompidou's successor to the presidency, in 1974, was greeted with anticipation and hope by Israel's friends. The centre-right politician had opposed the arms embargo and counted among his friends and associates such supporters of Israel as Michel Poniatowski and Jean Lecanuet. French Jews, who in great majority voted for the new President, were expecting a significant change in Middle Eastern policy promised during the election campaign.

Yet soon after the elections the policies of Giscard d'Estaing created disappointment. Although he lifted the arms embargo against Israel (by now the United States had become its principal arms supplier), he approved a Common Market declaration on the Middle East, stressing "Palestinian aspirations" to a state, and the French delegation to the U.N. backed a resolution to invite Yasser Arafat to the General Assembly. In November, 1974, the new Foreign Minister, Sauvagnargues, travelled to Beirut and became the highest ranking Western political figure to shake hands with the leader of the Palestine Liberation Organization.

President Giscard d'Estaing managed to placate the disheartened French Jews by receiving a delegation of the community's representatives in the Elysée Palace and by promising to intervene on Israel's behalf in negotiations over a Common Market trading agreement. But, a few months later the French government allowed the P.L.O. to open an information office in Paris, and in March of 1976 the French U.N. delegate, Louis de Guiringaud, announced in the Security Council France's unequivocal support for "the right of the Palestinian people to an independent state in Palestine." No other European state had gone as far in its backing of Arafat without asking him to give up terrorism or to modify the P.L.O. charter calling for the destruction of Israel. In 1978, Farouk Kaddoumi, the P.L.O.'s Marxist "Foreign Minister," praised the conservative French President as the leader of pro-P.L.O. activity in Europe. In 1979, plans to invite Arafat for an official visit to France were cancelled at the last moment only because of strong pressure from the Jewish community. By then twelve years after De Gaulle's attribution of Israeli policies to stereotyped Jewish behavior, French Jews came to view the pro-Arab policies as decisions affecting not only their sentimental homeland, but their own welfare as well.

On the economic front, Giscard d'Estaing deepened and diversified ties with the oil-rich Arab states. In 1975, his government sold Iraq a nuclear reactor capable of producing weapons-grade fuel. Although France claimed that it had obtained satisfactory safeguards against the utilization of this facility for military purposes, it gave in to the Iraqi demands for delivery of highly enriched uranium, suitable for the production of atomic bombs. It also turned a blind eye to the fact that Iraq purchased from Italy a special laboratory permitting it to further enrich the fuel supplied by France. To counter the claim that Iraq would be unable to produce the lethal weapon because it submitted to international inspection, the "father" of the French atomic bomb, Francis Perrin, remarked that Iraq could "any day" simply declare: "now, I refuse the controls of the International Atomic Energy Commission and I will use my enriched uranium as I please."[43]

Along with the aggressive business courtship of the Arabs went a heavy dose of political catering, which other major Western trading nations seemed able to avoid. The French Government showed an eagerness to abide by Arab wishes in applying anti-Israeli boycott provisions that affected French Jewry. The boycott stipulated that merchandise or products from a company employing Jews were forbidden in Arab countries. Although in June, 1977, the French parliament passed a law which stated that Arab boycotts that discriminate against French citizens of the Jewish faith were illegal, Giscard d'Estaing's government issued an administrative ruling a month later that over-rode the parliamentary law, "in the economic interest of France."

A second decree issued by his Prime Minister, Raymond Barre, allowed widespread violation of the law involving cases of blatant discrimination against French Jews. When a Syrian delegation to France expressed interest in purchasing films, on condition that they not be produced with the participation of Jewish film makers, Alain Peyrefitte, Minister of Justice, promptly referred to the "Barre Decree" to facilitate the sale. In addition, the Franco-Arab chamber of commerce authenticated certificates showing that French firms were "innocent" of dealing with Israel, or that they were not employing Jewish executives. Knowing that their lucrative transactions were protected by the umbrella of official "exemptions," French companies readily complied with the provisions of the Arab boycott. A Jewish graduate of France's foremost institution for training high-level civil servants, the "Ecole Nationale de l'Administration," was informed by a major, government-owned company, that his presence was undesirable because, in the words of the company's president, "if we hire a Jewish executive, we will risk being boycotted by our Arab partners."[44] In another instance, a Jewish senior engineer of a company trading with Lebanon was asked to "remove himself" from negotiating a contract because "of the origin of his parents," even though the Lebanese did not insist on it.[45]

Commenting on a pro-Arab speech made by Giscard d'Estaing

during his March, 1980, visit to Jordan, a Jewish community leader described it as the "culmination of a long process of an alignment of French views with the most intransigent Arab view." He added, betraying the Jews' frustration: "there is something extravagant, unjust and intolerable in the President's position."[46] The "Renouveau Juif" ("Jewish Renewal") movement called for a "censure vote" against Giscard d'Estaing in the 1981 presidential election. After losing his bid for re-election Giscard d'Estaing complained that Jewish journalists led a campaign against him.[47]

In 1980, a European conference on terrorism denounced France's tolerant attitude toward terror organizations. Paliamentarians, jurists and security experts accused France of inactivity against terrorism and claimed that it offered hospitality to certain kinds of terrorists. A British delegate, Paul Wilkinson, charged that "Paris had become the center of international terrorism" and that France failed to sign a Council of Europe agreement aimed at combatting terrorists.[48] A year earlier, an official of a police union accused the government and the police hierarchy of having turned a blind eye to the "activities of the militant extreme right" directed at Jews and immigrants.[49] The tolerant attitude to Middle Eastern terrorists coincided with a growth of Fascist and left-wing terrorism.

Few acts better characterized France's lax attitude toward terrorism than an incident involving the alleged mastermind of the murder of Israeli athletes at the 1972 Munich Olympics, Abou Daoud. When the P.L.O. official was arrested on French soil in January, 1977, under a standing Interpol warrant, both the Israeli and German governments asked for his extradition. However, French authorities quickly escorted the master terrorist to Algeria. Forgetting the P.L.O.'s highjacking of an Air France airliner to Entebbe a few months earlier, the French government, violated an extradition treaty with Israel to demonstrate its continued friendship toward the Arab world. A few newspapers deplored the immorality of the government decision. Others, like *Le Monde*, merely rebuked the authorities for creating a situation in which the judiciary appeared more accomodating to the government than the police. *Le Monde* made no reference to the expediency, to the desire not to offend Arab clients nor to disturb impending arms sales which prompted the French government to violate its own laws.

There were other instances of laxity toward terrorism: the

release of Iraqi "diplomats" who shot two French policemen on a busy Paris street, and the tolerance of the fact that some Arab embassies in Paris became safe havens and arms depots for terror organizations. At the same time, the French government did not pass up an opportunity to condemn Israel for pre-emptive or retaliatory actions after P.L.O. terror attacks on civilian targets. The author of a study of France's Middle Eastern policy concluded that the French "evinced a reluctance to condemn outrightly either highjackings by Arab guerillas or sabotage within Israel, on the grounds that such terrorism might be called legitimate action by an occupied people against a foreign power."[50]

It was consistent with its previous attitudes toward the Arab-Israeli conflict that France should express almost immediate scepticism toward what was to emerge as the Camp David process. Soon after Anwar Sadat's historic visit to Jerusalem in November, 1977, the Prime Minister, Raymond Barre, declared that "sentiments do not create policies." In *Le Monde* — which echoed the French Foreign Ministry's stand that only a "global" settlement would be acceptable — Sadat's visit was immediately branded as a "separate peace." Even in the final stages of the 1981 presidential campaign Giscard d'Estaing refused to endorse the Camp David agreements.

The effect of the anti-Israeli policies on the re-emergence of anti-Semitism in France was unmistakable. The former cabinet minister, Simone Veil, charged that governmental worsening of relations with Israel have permitted some people "to display their anti-Semitism nonchalantly."[51] Simone Veil's views were not isolated. The leader of a major teachers' union expressed the concern that "France is conducting an anti-Israeli policy which can create mass anti-Semitism."[52] In this climate of mutual accusations France's suspicions about its Jews were reflected in French Jewry's suspicions about France.

# Notes

[1]Jan. 8, 1969.
[2]*Le Canard enchaîné*, Jan. 15, 1969.
[3]P. Tesson in *Combat*, Jan. 8, 1969.
[4]Quoted in *Le Monde*, Jan. 9, 1969.
[5]On the popular "Europe No. 1" radio station, on Jan. 9, 1969.
[6]Quoted in Uri Dan, *L'Embargo* (Paris: Editions Premières, 1969), p. 163.
[7]Vincent Monteil, *Le Monde*, March 23-24, 1969.

[8]Claude Bourdet, "De Gaulle, Israël et l'antisémitisme," *Le Monde*, Jan. 17, 1969.

[9]Cohen, *De Gaulle*, p. 131.

[10]The article from *La Réforme* was partly reproduced in *Le Monde* on January 7, 1969.

[11]*Le Monde*, Jan. 19-20, 1969.

[12]Christian Perroux, *Nouveau Régime*, no. 5 (May, 1969). Quoted in Cohen, *De Gaulle*, p. 287.

[13]Cohen, *De Gaulle*, pp. 212-214.

[14]*Ibid.*, p. 214.

[15]Léon Noël, *Comprendre De Gaulle* (Paris: Plon, 1972), p. 301, quoted in Cohen, *De Gaulle*, p. 209. On Jewish denials of collusion in the referendum vote see J. Sabbath, "Y a-t-il un vote juif," *L'Arche* (June, 1969).

[16]Claude Bourdet, *Le Monde*, Jan. 1, 1970.

[17]Cohen, *De Gaulle*, p. 309.

[18]Michel Jobert, *L'Autre regard* (Paris: Grasset, 1976), p. 121.

[19]*Ibid.*, p. 133.

[20]P. de Saint Robert, *Les Septennats interrompus* (Paris: Laffont, 1977), p. 196.

[21]*Ibid.*, p. 269.

[22]On Dec. 19, 1969, Defense Minister Michel Debré denied the existence of negotiations, then reversed himself, adding that they involved "about fifteen" aircraft.

[23]Jobert, *L'Autre regard*, p. 137.

[24]See in particular *Le Monde*, Feb. 27, 1970.

[25]Pierre Rouanet, *Pompidou* (Paris: Grasset, 1969), p. 80.

[26]*Le Monde*, March 5, 1970.

[27]*The New York Times*, Feb. 26, 1970.

[28]*Ibid.*, March 3, 1970.

[29]Cohen, *De Gaulle*, p. 169.

[30]S.K. Crosbie, *A Tacit Alliance: France and Israel from Suez to the Six Day War* (Princeton, N.J.: Princeton University Press, 1974), p. 210.

[31]*Ibid.*

[32]"Union des Juifs pour la Résistance et l'Entreaide," *Le Monde*, March 27, 1970.

[33]*Le Monde*, March 15-16, 1970.

[34]*Le Monde*, March 15-16, 1970. From a statement by the "Union des Engagés Volontaires et Anciens Combattants."

[35]*Ibid.*, March 11, 1970.

[36]André Fontaine, "L'Ombre de l'affaire Dreyfus," *Le Monde*, March 15-16, 1970.

[37]Aron, *De Gaulle, Israël et les Juifs*, p. 24.

[38]*Le Monde*, Nov. 4, 1969.

[39]Edward J. Kolodziej, *French International Policy Under De Gaulle and Pompidou* (Ithaca and London: Cornell University Press, 1974), p. 502.

[40]C. Clément, *Israël et la Ve République* (Paris: Olivier Orban, 1978), p. 199.

[41]Quoted in Clément, *Israël et la Ve République*, p. 199.

[42]Cited by Cohen, *De Gaulle*, p. 176.

[43]Quoted in a letter to *Le Monde*, May 15, 1981.

[44]Harris and Sédouy, *Juifs et Français*, pp. 190-191.

[45]*Ibid.*, p. 338.

[46]H. Hajdenberg quoted in *Le Monde*, April 29, 1980.

[47]R. Liscia, *L'Arche* (November, 1980), p. 37.

[48]*Le Monde*, Nov. 15, 1980.

49J. Nodin, *Le Monde*, Oct. 17, 1980.
50Crosbie, *A Tacit Alliance*, p. 210-211.
51Veil's statement was reported in *Le Monde* on Oct. 9, 1980.
52André Henry quoted in *Libération*, Oct. 6, 1980.

# CHAPTER III

# Only Lice Were Gassed in Auschwitz

In the late 1970s, the passionate discussion of the rediscovered "Jewish question" led to a loosening of constraints on the use of anti-Semitic rhetoric in the daily press, in popular weeklies, on radio and on television. Under the guise of a highly publicised rediscovery of a painful segment of French history, the Vichy period, the media legitimized the discussion of any topic pertaining to the Jews and the Nazi period, without discriminating between historical analysis and a quest for curiosity laced with provocative sensationalism. By the middle of 1980, a point was reached where "not a week had passed without the appearance of an article in a major publication analyzing the conundrum of: French Jews; French *and* Jews; French *or* Jews?".[1]

Until the late 1970s, a myth that glorified the clandestine fight against the Germans was laboriously fostered by the various governments of the Fourth and Fifth Republics. The Resistance, the relatively small guerilla movement, was portrayed as a body representing a national consensus against the Germans. In reality, those involved in armed struggle against the occupiers constituted a relatively small group in which Communists and Jews were present in disproportionate numbers. On the other hand, far from being a band of quislings, the Vichy authorities ran the country with the approval of the vast majority of Frenchmen. Pétain's regime helped the German war machine, led a propaganda campaign against the Allies, recruited a French Division that fought on the Russian Front and initiated racist legislation that in some instances, exceeded in stringency equivalent German statutes. Yet for decades France's posture in World War II was glorified in the name of the Resistance, while the massive collaboration was remarkably absent from public discourse. There seemed to be a conspiracy of silence on Vichy's disgraceful record. The French resisted coming to terms with the unpleasant facts, and chief among them was Vichy's treatment of the Jews. It came, therefore, as somewhat of a surprise when the issue was flung with unusual fanfare upon French public opinion by a popular magazine.

The headline, "Only Lice Were Gassed in Auschwitz," in the largest-circulation French weekly, was meant to be sensational. In the fall of 1978, L'Express carried a long interview with the former "Commissioner for Jewish Affairs" in the Vichy government.[2] If the front cover caption was provocative, the subheadings in the story were hardly less shocking: "The disappearance of six milion Jews? An invention, pure and simple! A Jewish invention!," "Regrets? regrets for what?" The interview with the unrepentant "French Eichmann," Louis Darquier de Pellepoix, who was living in exile in Spain, was printed without any editorial comment, without any indication of disapproval or disbelief. The sheer violence of Darquier's anti-Semitic rhetoric, absent from the French press for over three decades, came as a shock because few imagined that such crude anti-Semitic language, even in the form of a historical reportage, could find its way into the pages of a liberal mass-circulation news magazine.

The unease grew among those who realized that Darquier's lies, exaggerations and half-truths were aimed at the young generation of French men and women, unencumbered by the skeletons in their parent's closets and often brought up on a heavy dose of left-wing anti-Zionism. The old Nazi used the mass-media forum given to him to portray himself as a wise patriarch addressing the "misguided" and "inexperienced" French youth, which had been "taken in" by the Jews. Notable in his responses to the interviewer's questions were numerous canards about Jewish behavior and the "Jewish character."

From the very beginning of the interview Darquier told the readers of L'Express that the disappearance of six million Jews was a hoax, a Jewish invention prompted by a craving for notoriety and pity: "Jews are like that, they are ready to do anything for the sake of some publicity . . . they will do anything to obtain some pity." Darquier explained that the photographs of piles of underwear in concentration camp warehouses were faked, "but what do you expect, that is the way the Jews are, they must always lie." In response to the reporter's mention of a document which showed that his zeal exceeded even that of Eichmann's representatives in France, he commented: "It's a fake fabricated after the war by the Jews! Ah, these Jews...they are capable of anything in order to find a scapegoat." Referring to the pre-World War II immigration of Jews to France, Darquier played on French xenophobia to elicit understanding for his actions: "these foreigners, these half-breeds, these thousands of stateless individuals who were at the source of all our troubles; . . . these people who came to us from everywhere and anywhere, who wanted our ruin." He also prided himself on the fact that the French government never asked for his extradition, because, in his words, he was always "on the best of terms with the people in the French embassy in Madrid."

The man who was elected in 1935 to the Municipal Council of Paris on an anti-Semitic platform lectured the L'Express reporter: "You are too young, you don't know how matters were before the war;" "you have been intoxicated by Jewish propaganda." Darquier also found historical backing for his actions against Jews: "Already in the Middle Ages, the Occident, Christendom, fought against the tentacular incursions of the Jews. We did not invent the yellow star. If already in the twelfth century the Jews were forced to wear a round patch it is because there was a need for it." This veritable anthology of anti-Jewish myths inevitably evoked the theory of the Jewish "conspiracy" to dominate the world. "You must be blind," the old anti-Semite lectured the readers of L'Express, "you don't wish to understand that the Jews have only one idea in mind: to create trouble everywhere. For what purpose? You know it full well, to make Jerusalem the capital of the world." Not since World War II had any major publication in France printed such a compendium of anti-Semitic canards. The absence of explanatory notes and of a rebuttal compounded the deed.

In another context, and in a different format, this kind of diatribe could have been dismissed as an amusing historical curiosity. This interview would have been considered as a transcript of the bizarre ravings of an old Nazi collaborator. Appearing as it did, in an unedited form, in a respectable journal, Darquier's anti-Semitic diatribe seemed to contain a degree of credibility, especially in the eyes of the young, who did not experience the war period and were not taught in school about Vichy's treatment of the Jews. Moreover, the interview emerged at a time when doubts were being raised about other versions of recent history, and when the signs of a resurgence of both verbal and physical anti-Jewish activity were beginning to multiply.

According to the editor of L'Express, Jean-François Revel, the Darquier "affaire" was transformed into a "national psychodrama" and for months following the publication of the interview the press was full of stories about it. The editor of the weekly was compelled to set up an office to handle the flood of correspondence and telephone calls reacting to the interview.[3] Darquier de Pellepoix's utterances triggered a debate not only on the French role in the Holocaust, on French collaboration with the Germans, on the fact that some high Vichy officials were never purged and continued to hold senior public posts, but also on the "Jewish question" in general. Some well-known personalities protested the new journalistic licence for the publication of anti-Semitic rhetoric and expressed concern over the precedent set by L'Express. Regardless of the weekly's motivations, it was felt that putting the unedited, venomous, anti-Jewish sterotypes of an unrepentant Nazi in the spotlight of the highest circulation magazine in France, was irresponsible. Simone Veil, then Minister of Health, and a former inmate of Auschwitz, condemned the Darquier interview as "an attempt to make racists and Nazis look normal."[4]

Others felt, however, that L'Express had performed a service by stimulating a long-overdue self-examination of the Jewish issue. Raymond Aron, a member of the editorial board of L'Express, argued that the interview had only "disturbed those who do not wish to know or to remember."[5] The publicist, Jean-François Kahn, agreed that the publication of the L'Express document was "a good thing because it put everyone on guard."[6] Others hailed the "Affaire Darquier" as a milestone in the revision of the history of war-time collaboration and the persecution of the Jews.

There is no doubt that the L'Express interview thrust into broad daylight a taboo maintained for three decades. In the words of the editor of L'Express, for the first time since World War II French society "rediscovered on the popular level, on the level of mass culture, its anti-Semitic past."[7] For the first time young Frenchmen also learned that their country had been hiding the existence of "an authentically French anti-Semitism that was not dependent on German imports."[8] The debate brought into the open the fact that Vichy gave the Germans extensive assistance in solving "the Jewish problem," almost on the scale provided by the collaborationist governments in Rumania, Croatia, and Hungary. "Nothing could change the fact," wrote a prominent lawyer, "that the Vichy French State was anti-Semitic," and that this fact was translated into "effective assistance in the genocide of the Jews."[9] The Darquier interview revealed to the young generation that "the scoundrels were not only the Nazis, but also our fathers, our

uncles, our families, our neighbors, and that yesterday's scoundrels are still among us."[10]

At the same time, the interview created "an emotional shock
that swept everything away,"[11] that removed inhibitions against
public utterance of the growing chorus of denials of Hitler's
atrocity. At a time when many, especially the young, were becoming sceptical about history, "a doubt was planted in their minds,"
wrote a prominent columnist.[12] The young who have been lied to
so often in the past were made to doubt the dimensions and the
very reality of Hitler's crimes and of the existence of the gas
chambers. Now the young can say, he added, "it is true that Hitler
was somewhat crazy, but the Jews were his enemies, so he defended himself. He had a heavy hand, but after all war was war . . .
Historians, serious academics, explain that a great deal has been
exaggerated, and quite a bit invented. Darquier simply confirms
this . . . It is certain that he is not entirely wrong. There is something suspicious underneath."[13] The harmful effect of unedited
anti-Semitic rhetoric also had to be judged in the context of the
proliferation of other such material: "to the pamphlets, venomous
works, malicious articles that had hitherto emanated from semi-
clandestine sources, or from publications with a limited circulation, one must now add the key contribution supplied by
L'Express."[14]

The philosopher, V. Jankélévitch, remarked about the Darquier
interview that "sensationalism does not excuse everything," at a
time when "dormant instincts are coming awake and anti-
Semitism is returning to life."[15] The editor of L'Express himself
admitted, while defending his decision to print the interview, that
his magazine may have "reinforced in the minds of some a more
or less latent anti-Semitism . . . ." (Revel admitted later that had
he foreseen the reaction the interview would provoke, he would
have published it in a different form, prefaced by a detailed
explanatory article.)[16] The anti-Semites had been waiting for a
sign, wrote a French-Jewish lawyer. When they saw that it was
possible to utter with impunity from the pages of a well-known
weekly, that "only lice were killed in Auschwitz," they realized
that "a page had been turned...that the time had returned when
they can again speak out."[17]

Shortly after the publication of the interview with Darquier de
Pellepoix the writer Pierre Goldman, whose assassination a year
later was claimed by a right-wing organization, warned the Jews
of France of the new danger: "In this gentle France of 1978, let all

Jews, from the richest to the poorest, from the most assimilated to the outsider, from the least Jewish to the most Jewish, know that nothing is yet settled."[18] Goldman also warned of the increased dissemination of books denying the Holocaust. It did not take long for this concern to take on a new, much more disturbing aspect. Within a short time, the myth of the non-existence of Hitler's gas chambers moved to the pages of France's most prestigious daily.

A few weeks after the Darquier interview, Le Monde printed an article by a controversial lecturer of French literature at the University of Lyon, Robert Faurisson, entitled, "The Problem of the Gas Chambers, or the 'Rumor of Auschwitz'."[19] A notorious Holocaust denier, who had been convicted by French courts for defamation, Faurisson argued in his Le Monde article that Hitler's gas chamber never existed. Le Monde prefaced the article with a brief note justifying its decision to print it on educational grounds, in order to air the issue for the benefit of France's youth. The newspaper's editor explained that "the young generation is not given to accepting certain ideas without proof." Allegedly, such proof or lack of it, was to be adduced from Faurisson's article.

The Faurisson article claimed that the gas chambers in the concentration camps in Poland were invented by the Soviet and Polish "judicial propaganda." The article was copiously footnoted, and had the appearance of serious academic research, a format, one could argue, more likely to impress than to dissuade the young readers from believing the "revisionists' " lies. Faurisson's "evidence" came from allegedly "confidential" Red Cross documents and such "authoritative" sources as the former Commandant of Auschwitz, Höss, as well as from the American academic, A.R. Butz, the author of a book denying the Holocaust, The Hoax of the 20th Century. Throughout his article Faurisson used quotation marks for the terms "gas chamber" and "genocide." Very few of the young readers Le Monde was supposedly attempting to enlighten about the Holocaust were likely to have been familiar with the questionable nature of his sources. Some may have indeed accepted his ideas on the basis of the "proof" he presented.

On the same page of the issue, below Faurisson's "proof," Le Monde also published an article that was intended to serve as counter-evidence. Its author was identified as an official of the "Centre for Contemporary Jewish Documentation." In the minds of the skeptical young Frenchmen Le Monde was supposedly trying to educate, he may well have appeared merely as an employee of a

Jewish organization, a biased representative of the same Jewish "establishment" Faurisson accused of perpetuating the Holocaust "myth." Moreover, in contrast to the scholarly appearance of Faurisson's article, the rebuttal lacked footnotes and the information it contained could hardly appear more convincing to the young minds which, according to *Le Monde*, were "not given to accepting certain ideas without proof." *Le Monde's* objectivity appeared less than absolute. A human-rights organization, LICRA, sued *Le Monde* for printing Faurisson's "evidence." However, the measure of legitimacy granted to the "revisionist" historian by the fact that he obtained a forum for his views in France's most authoritative daily, could not be lessened by a court decision a few months later.

While most other West European countries, including West Germany, screened the NBC television dramatization of Hitler's mass murder, the series "Holocaust," hailed as a television event on both continents, all three government-controlled French TV networks initially turned it down, giving a variety of pretexts. The officials of TFI, the oldest of the three channels, scorned the American production as "fiction," and argued that there were "more serious ways of treating such a grave subject." (This same network had refused a few years earlier to screen an unflattering documentary on the occupation period, Marcel Ophuls' "The Sorrow and the Pity," which was acclaimed by television viewers in many Western countries.)[20] The second network, "Antenne 2," explained its refusal to show "Holocaust" by stating that it did not wish to devote airtime to the projection of a foreign film, since it was being urged to screen more French-produced material. The third network, "France 3," declared that budgetary problems, "insufficient funds," prevented it from purchasing "Holocaust." When the Polish-born artist and writer, Marek Halter, started a public subscription to assist the "impoverished" state-owned TV stations to acquire the NBC film, the authorities relented and the French public was eventually allowed to watch "Holocaust," after it was seen by most of Europe. However, the incident proved that in 1979 French sensitivities about the fate of the Jews in World War II were still high, and that there were still influential decision-makers in France who opposed the airing of the story about the Nazi atrocities for fear they might stir up further debate about the French role in it.

In contrast to reactions in other countries, the screening of "Holocaust" in France created considerable anti-Semitic ferment.

The network which showed the programme was inundated with phone calls branding "Holocaust" as Jewish propaganda. Callers were "scandalized," according to a network official, by the prominence and "exclusivity" given to Jewish suffering. Others commented that the film "resurrected" events from the past that ought to be forgotten, and that the series indicated that the Jews were still seeking revenge four decades later. A *Le Monde* commentator warned that the Jews' insistence on a "special commemoration" of the Holocaust would "in the end, isolate them."[21] He echoed the view that the production of a film series on a topic that "should be laid to rest," was proof of the Jews' vindictiveness.[22] A spokesman for the "New Right" questioned the uniqueness of the Holocaust: "the history we are living is not only that of the Hebraic tragedy...a report of Amnesty International shows that we cannot concentrate our denunciation of totalitarianism on a single aspect of horror."[23] The same sentiments were expressed in a leftist daily in overtly anti-Semitic terms: "the deportation of a bothersome minority [the Jews during the Hitler period], is not an exceptional event in history."[24]

Letters in the printed media contended that the television serial, "Holocaust," was a means of diverting world public attention from the Israelis' mistreatment of the Palestinians. Some readers seized the opportunity to raise the issue of the causes for the persecution of Jews, and implied that the Jews must have a share in the atrocities committed against them. A reader of *Le Monde* expressed his "disgust" at the "drubbing inflicted on France" in the media on the occasion of the screening of the NBC production. The reactions to the screening of "Holocaust" confirmed the persistence of a malicious, endemic ill-will toward Jews in France.

The comments of Education Minister Chistian Beullac, addressed to French pupils on the occasion of the screening of "Holocaust," confirmed the obstinate resistance to the notion of the uniqueness of the Jewish tragedy, even among the elite. Intimating that watching the NBC dramatization could be harmful to their sense of morality, the minister warned the young "to distinguish and choose in this fictional world."[25] Beullac also stressed that Hitler's genocide was not unique in history, that it was just "one genocide, one totalitarianism, in one region of the world."[26] The editorialist of the Jewish Telegraphic Agency in Paris noted that this attempt to compare other tragedies in history to the systematic extermination of six million Jews risked "normalizing" the Holocaust, and that the Minister of Education failed to allude to Vichy's heavy responsibility in the deportations to Auschwitz.

The Beullac statement, and other government reactions to the "discovery" of the Vichy period, prompted revelations that the regime of President Giscard d'Estaing was harboring a right-wing elite whose past was tainted; individuals who represented, socially and politically, a segment of the right-wing stratum that never completely rejected Vichy thinking. Some recalled the violent, but brief, indignation that followed, three years earlier, Giscard d'Estaing's unilateral decision to abolish the annual May 8 festivities celebrating the victory over Nazism. Charges were made that former militant Fascists and anti-Semites could still be found in the corridors of political power. These accusations were partially born out when, in the spring of 1981, evidence emerged that the Budget Minister Maurice Papon, had signed deportation papers against Jews while exercising his functions as Prefect of the Gironde region during the Occupation.

The revelation of many of these facts was followed by the public with detached curiosity. There were no demands for an investigation of war-time wrongdoing. On popular television programmes former Vichy notables, who seemed to have lost earlier inhibitions, voiced barely disguised old anti-Semitic notions. The commotion around the "Jewish question" seemed to stir up long-dormant sentiments and supplied grist for the anti-Semitic mill. "Now they think they can lower their masks and admit that they regret nothing," wrote a journalist in *Le Matin*, in reference to the brazen public behavior of former Vichy collaborators.[27]

It was not coincidental that, in 1978, the life-story of Hitler's mistress, Eva Braun, was programmed on national television and that the leading literary weekly, *Les Nouvelles littéraires*, published on its front page a crudely anti-Semitic letter by the novelist, Céline, a notorious admirer of Hitler, allegedly in the name of rediscovering history. At the same time, Parisian youths were adopting the swastika as a symbol of derision and books bearing such titles like, *The Memoirs of a Fascist* were beginning to crowd the shelves of bookstores. A literary critic observed that the publication of books with a pro-German bias or treating the German side of the Second World War had increased ten-fold in one year.[28] High-school teachers reported that students showed their interest in history by reading material about Nazis in magazines "that swarm with disturbing articles about the SS, the Gestapo, the Vichy militia."[29]

In this climate of apparent exoneration of war-time Fascism it came as almost no surprise when a Dean of Medicine at the University of Paris openly declared that he was a Fascist. The former member of the French SS Division, "Charlemagne," proudly declared in front of an academic gathering: "I was a Fascist and I remain a Fascist. Why is it a serious offense to be a Nazi? I do not understand why people could be shocked."[30] Even the popular, non-ideological press indulged in publishing anti-Semitic material. A Jewish activist charged that the Paris daily, *Le Parisien Libéré*, known as the newspaper of the "concierges," turned into an "anti-Semitic rag."[31]

Following the Darquier interview, a notorious admirer of Pétain was invited to appear on France's most-watched television literary programme, "Apostrophes." In spite of his tainted past, Alfred Fabre-Luce had become a fixture in the Parisian intellectual establishment and published regularly in *Le Monde* and *Le Figaro*. Shortly after the Darquier and "Holocaust" "affairs," Fabre-Luce rushed into print a book, *Pour en finir avec l'antisémitisme*[32] (*To be Done with Anti-Semitism*), in which he described the Darquier affair as a media event staged by the Jews in order to bring non-Jews "to contrition."[33] The uproar over the interview, Fabre-Luce wrote, proved the existence "of a special sort of justice exercised by the Jews."[34] The book itself became a "media event" and sparked debates in the press. Reviving the old anti-Semitic cliché of the vengeful Jew, Fabre-Luce wrote that Jewish "piety toward the dead is indistinguishable from a desire for vengeance."[35] Serge Klarsfeld, the well-known Nazi hunter, was motivated, according to Fabre-Luce, by "vengeance rather than justice."[36] An official of the Jewish community found it a "grave" matter that a former Vichy collaborator, who openly vents "rabid anti-Semitism," should receive exposure on such prestigious programmes as "Apostrophes."

Although he claimed he was "a friend of the Jews," Fabre-Luce suggested in his book that Jews must be held to account for "their part of responsibility in their misfortune,"[37] and claimed that they secretly wish to suffer.[38] Their religion, he wrote, has turned them into masochists: "a very ancient complex originating in the Jewish religion has created an intimate link between misfortune, vengeance and power."[39] In a rambling apology of the Vichy regime Fabre-Luce accused a Jewish "lobby" of distorting its record and argued that collaboration with the Nazis had allowed Pétain to limit the number of victims, "especially the number of

French victims."[40]

Fabre-Luce also blamed the Jews for the increase in anti-Semitism. By showing solidarity toward their brethren, by refusing to assimilate fully, Jews bring upon their heads persecutions, "they expose themselves to reactions that ghetto Jews encountered in the past."[41] To prove his point he quoted former Austrian Chancellor Bruno Kreisky, the foremost example of a self-hating Jew in our time, to the effect that assimilation is "the only true solution, to the Jewish issue."[42] In the view of Fabre-Luce, to be allowed to live in a country like France Jews must abandon their particularism, renounce their ancient collective memory and their empathy with the State of Israel. They must also abstain from criticizing government policies favorable to the Arab states. Stirring up controversy over Vichy, Fabre-Luce implied, was part of a Jewish plot to rewrite history and an Israeli-inspired strategy to put moral pressure on pro-Arab Europeans.

Other well-known media figures expressed a willingness to accept the public discussion of the fate of the Jews during the occupation, provided that the debate not be limited to crimes against Jews. The editor of *Le Monde*, Jacques Fauvet, expressed concern, in a front-page editorial, that the media give themselves "a good conscience by deploring the long-passed deportation of Jews," while forgetting "the more recent atrocities of the Algerian drama."[43] By comparing Hitler's methodical genocide to the atrocities committed by both sides during the war in Algeria in the 1950s, Fauvet joined the growing trend to trivialize the significance of the Holocaust. *Le Monde's* editor also warned against the neglect of "all forms of racism," a code-word of the French left negating the primacy of anti-Jewish prejudice. Fauvet typified those pundits, "'above all suspicion', who were willing to discuss the Holocaust on the condition that no aspect of contemporary reality be neglected."[44] His views exemplified those of the many commentators who expounded a " 'universally anti-racist' discourse by establishing immediate comparisons...and spoke only of 'Holocausts' in the plural under the pretext that the word 'genocide' is not uniquely 'Jewish'."[45]

In the wake of these debates attention was focused on a former high Vichy official, Jean Leguay, whose responsibility seemed particularly heavy and who had pursued, unmolested, a lucrative career in international business after serving in various government posts since 1945. During the war, Leguay was the top police authority in the "occupied zone" and was involved in the July,

1942, roundup of Paris Jewry. Demanding that Leguay be indicted for crimes against humanity, Serge Klarsfeld (who together with his wife Beate tracked down Klaus Barbie and was instrumental in bringing to justice several notorious German war criminals), presented documented evidence that the zeal of this French police official exceeded even that of Gestapo officers. Yet, after the war, Leguay was whitewashed by a special tribunal because he allegedly saved some French Resistance members as well as a few Jews. In 1946, he was sent on an official mission to the United States. Subsequently, the man who, Klarsfeld charged, was "one of the organizers of the genocide," "who planned the arrests, the deliveries and the departures of the trains," was allowed to live in luxury in Paris for three decades.

Faced with the publicity surrounding them, French Jews were on the horns of a dilemma. On one hand, they feared the re-emergence of the "ugly beast" from the past, and wished that the commotion would subside; and on the other, they were anxious to keep alive the memory of the Hitler period. The author of an article in a Jewish monthly echoed part of this predicament: "Have we reached the foreboding hour when one worries about an upcoming resurgence and the means to counter it? ... The hour when one happily feels like the only survivor of an air crash and at the same time the only one who is being flayed alive in a joyful crowd?"[46] The wide publicity given to the claims of falsifiers of Holocaust history turned what was considered an aberrant, fringe phenomenon into a topic worthy of serious debate. The political historian, Blandine Barret-Kriegel, observed that while there exist Holocaust doubters like Faurisson in countries other than France, "nowhere else have their theories been as widely circulated as in France, where the views of a Faurisson have been received rather favorably."[47]

In this atmosphere, anti-Semitic literature written before the war was beginning to be discussed in a manner that reduced racial loathing to a sort of estheticism. By 1978, the writings of the long-dead novelist, Louis-Ferdinand Céline, a pathological Jew-hater, were hailed on television programmes as poetic, and the novelist Drieu de la Rochelle, a notorious collaborator during the war, was praised for his talent. Television literary experts, were carrying on, in the words of a noted columinist, "salon conversations in the shadow of crematoria."[48] In the august French Academy, the former Minister of Justice, Alain Peyrefitte, a member of the Academy, praised the talent of Paul Morand, a writer who served in the Vichy government and who had openly expressed the desire for a German victory.

Not unrelated to the recognition of the esthetic merits of former Nazi collaborators was a denunciation of the ethics of Judaism. In a prestigious intellectual publication a rising star on the Paris literary scene, J.-E. Hallier, called for the "destruction of metaphysical Judaism" in the name of a new pagan ideology.[49] A Jewish thinker observed that these "disturbing words reflected the current state of anti-Semitism in France."[50]

The review of the occupation period events was accompanied by the emergence of a wave of World War II nostalgia, which manifested itself through the so-called "retro" fashion in clothing and in films. Slick, dark overcoats worn by the Gestapo, wardrobes and haircuts popular with the shady underworld that dominated social life in occupied France, were paraded by mannequins of Parisian high-fashion houses. The new wave in the cinema indulged in a nostalgic glance back to the war-time years and created sympathetic portrayals of characters who a few years earlier would have aroused revulsion. In the movies of the late 1970s concentration-camp life became the arena of sado-masochistic adventures, in which morbidity seemed to serve as a stimulus to a novel sort of sexual escapade. The reading public thirsted for biographies of Nazi celebrities and showed an avid curiosity for books dealing with the Hitler period. In this climate "the right to baseness could finally be recognized!"[51]

It is also this atmosphere which allowed a Faurisson to emerge as a semi-credible historian. Somehow, in the new social environment that favored psychoanalysis and mysticism, Faurisson's contention that the figure of six million dead was the product of a "Talmudic propensity" to mathematical exaggeration, did not appear so far-fetched. His claims that the main villain of the 1930s and 1940s was Stalin, not Hitler, echoed with a measure of credibility in a society that seemed suddenly to discover the existence of the Soviet Gulags (following the translation into French of Solzhenitsyn's work). To the mind of a young Frenchman, bewildered by the downfall of ideologies, of long-held beliefs, was it really unreasonable to claim, as seemingly respectable journalists did, that the "repatriation" of the Jews to "relocation camps" in their "countries of origin" in the East, was akin to the resettlement of Algerians by the French government in 1961?

In the late 1970s, following Solzhenitsyn's revelations about Soviet barbarism, the intellectual crisis experienced by the young leftist generation created a confusion of values and of terminology. The term "racism" acquired a universal meaning. New adjectives were attached to it: "anti-old," "anti-young" or "anti-feminist." French policemen dispersing crowds were called "SS," "Assassins" and the term "genocidal" was frequently applied to Israeli preemptive attacks on Palestinian terrorist bases. The dissemination of the belief that anti-Zionism, even in its most crudely anti-Semitic form, was just another anodine political opinion, and that anti-Semitism could be interpreted as the expression of hatred toward capitalism,[52] led to a loosening of taboos, and to the defamation of the memory of the victims of Hitler's crimes.[53]

# Notes

[1]Shimon Samuels, "Anti-Semitism in France: Roots and Consequences," *ADL International Report* (June, 1980), p. 1.

[2]"A Auschwitz, on n'a gazé que les poux," Oct. 28 - Nov. 4, 1978, pp. 164-99.

[3]In an interview with this writer in May, 1983.

[4]In a broadcast on the radio station "Europe I" on Oct. 30, 1978.

[5]*L'Express*, Nov. 11-18, 1978, p. 119.

[6]*L'Express*, Nov. 4-11, 1978, p. 112.

[7]J-F. Revel, "Fin d'un tabou," *L'Arche* (Sept.-Oct., 1979), p. 71. For a comprehensive review of Vichy's attitude to Jews see, Michael R. Marrus and Robert O. Paxton, *Vichy France and the Jews*. New York: Basic Books, 1981.

[8]Revel, *L'Arche* (Sept.-Oct., 1979).

[9]Robert Badinter, "Pour un jugement des crimes contre l'humanité," *Le Monde*, June 15, 1979 (Badinter became Minister of Justice in the Mitterrand administration).

[10]Serge July, *Libération*, Nov. 6, 1978.

[11]J. Sabbath, "Fin d'un tabou," *L'Arche* (Sept.-Oct., 1979), p. 71.

[12]P. Viansson-Ponté in a letter to *L'Express*, Nov. 15-25, 1978, p. 239.

[13]*Ibid.*

[14]*Ibid.*

[15]*Le Matin*, Nov. 1, 1978.

[16]J-F. Revel, *L'Arche* (Sept.-Oct., 1979), p. 73. The second thoughts about the format of the publication were revealed by Revel to this writer in May, 1983.

[17]Jean Bloch-Michel, "Anti-Semitism and the French 'New Right'," *Dissent* (Summer, 1980), p. 291.

[18]*Libération*, Oct. 31, 1978.

[19]*Le Monde*, Dec. 29, 1978.

[20]"The Sorrow and the Pity" was finally approved for television viewing by the Mitterrand administration in November, 1981.

[21]Gilbert Comte, *Le Monde*, March 14, 1979.

[22]*Ibid.*

[23]Louis Pauwels, "Un Terrorisme peut en cacher un autre," *Le Figaro-magazine*, Feb. 10, 1979.

[24]P. Guillaume in *Libération*, March 7, 1979, quoted by J. Tarnero in *L'Arche* (February, 1981), p. 17.

[25]*Le Monde*, Feb. 16, 1979.

[26]*Ibid.*

[27]J.-F. Kahn, *Le Matin*, Nov. 1, 1978.

[28]B. Poirot-Delpech, *Le Monde*, Dec. 29, 1978.

[29]N. Drouin and J. Assaël, "Banalisation ou oubli: est-ce le seul dilemme?," *Les Nouveaux cahiers*, no. 56 (Spring, 1979), p. 33.

[30]*Le Monde*, March 28, 1979.

[31]Pierre Goldman, in *Libération*, Nov. 6, 1978.

[32]Paris: Julliard, 1979.

[33]*Pour en finir avec l'antisémitisme*, p. 104. Describing the 1940 exodus of refugees fleeing from Hitler's armies, Fabre-Luce remarked that those running away included not only Jews but "all those they corrupted or seduced." He also referred to Jewish refugees on a ship as cowards "seeking shelter behind Christians like a negro King behind hostages." (*Journal de France, Mars 1939-Juillet 1940*, Paris: Imprimerie de Trévoux, 1940, pp. 395, 378).

[34]*Ibid.*, p. 131.

[35]*Ibid.*, p. 106.

[36]*Ibid.*, p. 108.

[37]*Ibid.*, p. 11.

[38]*Ibid.*, p. 59.

[39]*Ibid.*, p. 134.

[40]*Ibid.*, p. 100.

[41]*Ibid.*, p. 109.

[42]*Ibid.*, p. 133.

[43]*Le Monde*, Nov. 14, 1978.

[44]Drouin and Assaël, *Les Nouveaux cahiers*, no. 56, pp. 33-34.

[45]*Ibid.*

[46]F. Rohman, "Les Quittances d'Hitler," *Les Nouveaux cahiers*, no. 56 (Spring, 1979), p. 17.

[47]"Derapage de la gauche?," *Les Nouveaux cahiers*, no. 71, p. 13.

[48]Claude Sarraute, *Le Monde* Dec. 3, 1978. Cited in J. Tarnero, "Adolf et les chics types," *Les Nouveaux cahiers*, no. 64 (Spring, 1981), p. 29.

[49]*Art press international* (March, 1979). See chapter VI on the significance of this "New Right" ideology.

[50]S. Trigano, "Les 'nouveaux' racistes et Hallier," *Esprit*, no. 5 (May, 1979), p. 121.

[51]Tarnero, *Les Nouveaux cahiers*, no. 64, p. 28.

[52]Andreas Baader, the leader of the German left-wing terror group, the "Baader-Meinhof Gang," expressed this view in an interview he gave in prison shortly before his death, thus resurrecting the beliefs of some nineteenth-century socialists.

[53]Tarnero, *Les Nouveaux cahiers*, no. 64, p. 28.

# CHAPTER IV

# From Words to Violence

Through the late 1970s the French public, and many in the Jewish community, did not seem to be aware that sporadic anti-Jewish violence had been occurring for years. In 1975, a bomb seriously damaged the orthodox "Rashi" synogogue in Paris. The night-time blast went almost unnoticed. A year later a powerful explosive device was defused in front of the residence of the Chief Rabbi of France. By the spring of 1978, the proliferation of anti-Semitic incidents attracted the attention of *L'Express*. The weekly reported that in several large cities, in Dijon, Strasbourg and Marseilles, Jews were being harrassed by anonymous phone calls and affronted daily by such graffiti as "may Jewish blood flow again" and "the only good Jew is a Jew in the oven."[1]

Following the 1978 interview with the exiled "French Eichmann" and the projection of the NBC television programme, "Holocaust," anti-Semitic attacks began to occur with greater frequency. In March, 1979, thirty Jewish students were injured, some of them seriously, by a bomb blast in a kosher cafeteria near the Sorbonne. A month later, during a Jewish film festival, bombs were set to explode in front of a Paris cinema and Molotov cocktails were thrown at a Jewish lodging house and a synagogue. These actions were claimed by a group calling itself "The French Fighters against Jewish Occupation."

That same year, an explosion destroyed the car of the Nazi hunter, Serge Klarsfeld, and Pierre Goldman, the author of *The Obscure Memoirs of a Polish Jew Born in France*, was shot in broad daylight on a Paris street. The murder was claimed by a right-wing group. (A year earlier, in May 1978, a Jewish leftist, Pierre Curiel, was assassinated by a right-wing group calling itself "Honor of the Police." Curiel's widow received calls from individuals denouncing "international Jewry"). There was also an attempt on the life of the Jewish president of the League of

Human Rights, reports of numerous mail and telephone threats to well-known Jewish personalities, and many acts of vandalism against Jewish institutions, businesses and cemeteries.

Concern over mounting anti-Semitism was expressed by the daughter of a Jewish novelist who had converted to Catholicism in the thirties. In poignant terms she conveyed the depth of her anguish in a *Le Monde* article entitled, "We Are Afraid": "For several months now we have been attacked on all sides, and I wish to say it very loudly, that I feel this violence like a rape."[2] Elisabeth Gille, the daughter of Irène Nemirovsky, wrote that since the Darquier de Pellepoix interview in *L'Express*, she had felt assaulted by the sensation-seeking debates in the media and the display of provocative book titles on the "Jewish question." She also depicted the atmosphere in her son's Paris high school: the suffering and the fear experienced by Jewish students, the Nazi slogans covering the walls, the excrement deposited in front of the Jewish chapel, and the children's pleas to their teachers for protection. A teacher who objected to a student wearing a Nazi uniform in class and to the portrait of an S.S. officer on a wall was subjected to insults. Elisabeth Gille called for an examination of "today's anti-Semitism" in French society and for measures of protection for her children. A few weeks later, another newspaper reported the story of a Jewish pupil in a private school who had been repeatedly tortured and humiliated by his classmates.

In 1979, the authors of *Juifs et Français*, a probing study of the condition of French Jewry, André Harris and Alain de Sédouy, wrote that attacks on Jewish property were no longer counted. Anti-Semitic graffiti in the Paris subway, on buses and on sidewalks became a common sight. Even the tombstones of Canadian Jewish soldiers, who fell for the liberation of France in World War II, were smashed at a military cemetery in Normandy. In June 1980, the Saint-Paul district in Paris, the old Jewish "pletzl," was the scene of an attack that recalled the horrors of the past. About 40 neo-Nazis, shouting "death to the Jews, kill them," wearing helmets and arm bands with swastikas, ran through the neighborhood attacking everyone in sight. They chased the Jews in what was described as a "real manhunt." Armed with iron bars and brass knuckles they beat and terrorized the residents of the old Jewish neighborhood.

In late September, four Jewish communal structures in Paris, a day school, a nursery, a memorial to the victims of the Holocaust and a synagogue, were hit with machine-gun fire. If in the past, the anti-Jewish attacks seemed haphazard and un-coordinated, this time the targets were carefully selected to make the greatest impact, to arouse distress and anxiety in as many segments of the Jewish community as possible. Fearing for the lives of their children, the parents of a large Jewish day school in Paris collected funds to install an elaborate television surveillance system, bullet-proof doors and windows throughout the building.

In 1980, on one of the most important dates in the Jewish calender, on the festival known as the "Rejoicing of the Torah," a powerful explosion shook the rue Copernic Liberal synagogue in Paris. The bomb was timed to kill scores of worshippers at the moment they were to emerge from the sanctuary following the holiday services. Only a fortuitous delay in the service prevented mass murder in the crowded temple. Yet the shock and the grief over the four dead victims could not be measured numerically. Few other incidents in recent experience have had a greater impact on the French Jewish community. Raymond Aron called it an "historical event." On October 3rd 1980, for the first time since the Holocaust, in a Western democracy, there was an attempt to kill Jews at prayer. Nothing could change this fact; not that, ironically, three of the four passers-by killed were not Jewish, nor that the killers could have come from the ranks of Palestinian, neo-Nazi, or left-wing terrorist groups.

The uncertainty about the identity of the terrorists did not change the significance of the act itself. For above all, the explosion in the fashionable "Etoile" district of Paris demonstrated the dangers of complacency in the face of mounting verbal and physical anti-Semitic violence. The explosion showed how the inevitable logic of escalation can lead from the abandonment of taboos on verbal anti-Semitism to the shedding of the final restraint which had previously discouraged even the most extremist elements from murdering Jews engaged in a prayer service. The ominous symbolism of the act escaped no one's attention. Because the Jews had again become the target of public vilification, the terrorists assumed that their acts were not in total disharmony with a public opinion that had not condemned previous, less dramatic attacks. Two years after the tragic event, a French-Jewish philosopher pointed out the implications of the rue Copernic bombing: "it suddenly revealed to the Jews, not through the symbolism of words but through a concrete act, their frightening precariousnesss in France . . . in spite of the horrors of Auschwitz, in spite of the establishment of an independent Jewish state."[3]

"The authors of this crime assumed that the moment to act was propitious," wrote the editor of a Paris newspaper three days after the explosion, adding, significantly, that the crime of rue Copernic "would have been unthinkable two years earlier."[4] The former president of the French League of Human Rights commented that the explosion revealed "the fact that today anti-Semites declare themselves openly...." The new element was not "so much the re-emergence of anti-Semitism as the creation of a new atmosphere."[5]

The cool, almost insulting response of the Giscard d'Estaing government to the rue Copernic synagogue bombing added to the anguish of the Jewish community. In a monumental slip of the tongue, Prime Minister Raymond Barre, expressed regret that the terrorists "intended to kill Jews, but wound up killing innocent Frenchmen" instead. The "unfortunate" wording, as his spokesman called it, added insult to injury, quite literally. The Barre miscue served as a reminder that in a country where several generations of elites were raised in an atmosphere of fashionable anti-Semitism even carefully phrased official statements can betray a subconscious prejudice. A prominent Jewish lawyer suggested that the Prime Minister's slip of the tongue proved that "his unconscious alone spoke for him." He also observed with sadness "the ease with which the sentiment that Jews are 'others' can be reborn, and that it behooves one not to be identified with them."[6] For another commentator, the implication of the Prime Minister's "gaffe" was unmistakeably racist: "those passing in the street were French and innocent, those praying in the synagogue were strangers and guilty."[7]

The President himself waited five days to make a statement to the nation. When it finally came it did not address the most pressing need of the moment: a warm, sympathetic gesture toward the Jewish community and a forthright denunciation of anti-Semitism by name. Instead, the French President's brief address, while containing a condemnation of the "criminal act," seemed to put greater stress on a denial of the existence of anti-Semitism (except among "small entrenched groups"), a defense of the police against accusations of laxity and a warning to the Jews against using counter-violence.

The synagogue bombing induced poignant anguish among Jews. "I feel like weeping out of rage,"[8] exclaimed Jean-Pierre Pierre-Bloch, a Jewish parliamentarian and a member of the ruling majority. A high school student told a reporter that the event affected everyone in the Jewish community, collectively and individually. The young Jew expressed fear and urged everyone to "demonstrate, shout and descend to the street by the millions."[9] Another eighteen year-old student wrote: "I am disappointed and ashamed; ashamed of believing even for a moment those people who where telling me that I was French, . . . ashamed of being proud of a country that may support me but does not love me...no one will ever fool me again."[10] Others expressed their anger by demonstrating a new sense of identity with fellow Jews. A former militant leftist attending a memorial service the day after the bombing remarked: "the Fascists have succeeded where my parents have failed: here I am on a Saturday morning in a synagogue, wearing a skull cap on my head."

The new Jewish consciousness was symbolized by the appearance of a button, "Juif de France" (French Jew), marking the distinction from the more assimilationist, "Français Juif" (Jewish Frenchman). The usually mild-mannered and cautious leader of the Jewish community, Baron Alain de Rothschild, blamed both the perpetrators of the crime and the authorities; he denounced "this last stage in an escalation" of anti-Semitic agitation, and the "indifference of our rulers." He also publicly dropped his previous opposition to the formation of Jewish self-defence units and echoed complaints about the inexplicable impotence of the police against Jew-hating extremists.

The CRIF (the French acronym for the "Representative Council of Jewish Institutions of France"), the central political body of French Jewry, presided over by Alain de Rothschild, issued a condemnatory statement that contained an exposition as well as an analysis of the situation: "the community addresses itself to the President of the Republic to deplore the passivity of the authorities in the face of international terrorism and attacks that have been directed at Jews for several years. This attitude led to the tragedy of the rue Copernic synagogue . . . it also led the terrorists to believe that they could act with total impunity against the Jewish community and Israel. One should not be surprised to see the Neo-Nazis raise their heads, openly proclaim their sinister doctrine...after the release of Abou Daoud, after an inefficient investigation of the murderous explosion in the Médicis restaurant, after a total absence of official reaction at the assassination in Antwerp of a Jewish child from Paris...."[11]

The eloquent "new philospher," Bernard-Henri Lévy, attributed the synagogue bombing to years of tolerance for re-emerging racist activity. The explosion was brought about, he claimed, by "a climate, an accumulation of political signs that we have been following with anxiety for a year or two." One cannot allow, he added, the "rehabilitation of old racial doctrines to go unpunished...without having one day to pay the consequences... bombs are never dropped without intent."[12]

A Canadian reporter visiting Paris several months after the bombing told a haunting story of an old Jewish couple that seldom unlocked the door of their apartment. Except for food deliveries their door was kept locked at all times. A neighbor speculated that perhaps the old Jews have "too many memories." The Toronto *Globe and Mail* reporter concluded philosophically: "from such vignettes is history made to come alive. In Paris, 1981 two old Jews are frightened once again."

Michael Williams, the British-born Rabbi of the rue Copernic synagogue, put his finger bluntly on what he considered to be the source of the evil that brought about the bombing: "the cancer of anti-Semitism that gnaws France." The Rabbi added that it "mattered little who actually set the bomb... the real problem for Jews in this country remains the same: it is this visceral, permanent distinction between Jews and Frenchmen."[13] The Rabbi and his congregants could only have been outraged by the demands of some shopkeepers on the rue Copernic that the synagogue compensate them for the damage caused by the blast. The symbolism of this callous attitude evoked the cruelest memories. The philosopher, Shmuel Trigano, also pointed to the endemic nature of French anti-Semitism: "the positive aspect of Jewish existence is forbidden in France."[14]

Well-known political figures also spoke out about the resurgence of anti-Semitism in France. Simone Veil recalled her own childhood and revealed that in nursery, when she was only four, she was already called a "dirty Jewess." Although she had been in the public eye for many years she had never previously discussed her own experience with anti-Semitism. The bombing of the synagogue brought forth, however, some deeply felt memories about her childhood: "all Jewish mothers dreaded the moment when their child would return from school and say, 'they called me a dirty Jew'."[15] Although she had held a cabinet post in the Giscard d'Estaing administration, Simone Veil charged that the Government's pro-Arab policies were stirring up antagonism against French Jews, and that the manner in which they were carried out blurred distinctions between hostility to Israel and to the Jewish people as a whole: "when an ambiguity is allowed to float, when some anti-Israeli attacks are in fact anti-Semitic, when one mixes such a policy with the situation of Jews in France, one creates anti-Semitism."[16]

Daniel Mayer, also a former cabinet minister, wrote in a similar vein: "the scorn of French political leaders toward Israel, their preference for a barrel of oil over a Jew, their betrayal and abandonment of Israel, contributed to making the Jew a being who stands apart,...a being below the general esteem.... To the extent that the teaching of scorn in Christian catechism has diminished... it has been replaced by a scorn of a political nature."[17]

The stream of statements, counter-statements and commentary that followed the rue Copernic explosion revealed the existence in France of a wide-spread network of interrelated factors pointing to the continued existence of a deeply entrenched animosity to Jews. Although there no longer existed any major political group espousing Judeophobia, no visible, overt "structures of receptiveness" for militant anti-Semitism as was the case in the past[18], it became apparent that the third-largest Diaspora in the world was facing a situation markedly different from other Jewish concentrations in Western democracies.[19] The trail led from De Gaulle's hostile attitude toward Israel and signals fostering suspicions about the loyalty of Jews, to the calculated obliviousness to terrorism of his successors and to police ineptitude in apprehending perpetrators of anti-Semitic acts. "The thunder has been audible for some time," wrote an indignant columnist, "yet we did not want to hear it." Where was public opinion, he asked, "who shouted 'no' after the bomb in the student restaurant, the destruction of stores, in the face of assaults against men, women, and Jewish children, because they were Jewish?"[20] The spotlight also fell on both extremes, of the left and of the right, that often fed on each other's enmity toward Jews and Zionism.

The massive demonstration through the streets of Paris, organized by the opposition parties after the rue Copernic bombing, seemed to indicate that many French people were opposed to anti-Semitism and were eager to express their sympathy to the Jewish community. It was significant that Frenchmen of diverse political streams united to walk under the same banner opposing racism. However, it soon became apparent that not all the marchers were motivated by abhorrence of anti-Semitism. The crowds and the slogans did not disguise the fact that the condemnation of anti-Semitism was not unequivocal.

Because the call for the demonstration first came from the Communist-led MRAP (Movement Against Racism and for Friendship of Peoples), some organizations, notably the moderate Socialist labor union, "Force Ouvrière," warned against joining in with those who thrive upon a tense climate and aim to "split republican institutions." Others, who hesitated to participate in the march feared that the largest labor union, the Communist-led C.G.T., and the Communist Party would dominate the demonstration and exploit it for their own political purposes. The highly publicized appeal to protest the bombing reminded observers that both the C.G.T. and the Communists were experts at organizing mass gatherings, and often utilized their apparatus for this purpose. Fearing political exploitation by the Marxists, the R.P.R., the party of Paris Mayor, Jacques Chirac, at first warned against participation: "in such a grave matter any political exploitation would be shameful...."In the end the neo-Gaullists also joined the march, fearful of political fallout.

In calling on members to participate in the demonstration, Communist leaders emphasized that they viewed the event as a stand against "all Fascist and racist activities" and against "violence directed at workers." The word anti-Semitism was never mentioned and the reference to "all racisms" was given to conjecture and implied that the Communists were reluctant to march on behalf of Jews alone. The mention of "workers" was a more direct allusion to the growing racism against Arab migrant laborers than to attacks on Jews. The placards, "Against all Racisms," also contained a coded message implying a condemnation of Zionism, branded as racist by Communist and Arab propaganda, particulary since the 1975 United Nations resolution that equated Zionism with racism. Some noted that the demonstration also gave the Communist Party the opportunity to respond to criticism about its lack of condemnation of Soviet anti-Semitism.

A keen observer of the French-Jewish scene noted later: "the most astonishing fact about this mass demonstration was that it blotted out the Jew . . . by not recognizing openly the Jew as the victim." Arnold Mandel labeled the demonstration as a "theatrical performance," as a "farce," that ought to have been denounced at the outset by the Jewish community. Mandel recalled, in another context, that the demonstrations and counter demonstrations that took place during the Dreyfus Affair were not motivated by purely humanitarian concerns. He cited, Bernard Lazare, the

Jewish writer who took up the defense of Captain Dreyfus, to the effect that the "Dreyfusards," the supporters of Dreyfus, often marched in demonstrations "only on their own behalf."[21]

Since the demonstration was held in an election year (banners denouncing police laxity and calls for the resignation of Interior Minister, Bonnet, were prominent), there was little doubt that it was exploited for political aims. Following François Mitterrand's election to the Presidency in May, 1981, many commentators agreed that the rue Copernic bombing and its political exploitation played an important part in the results of the ballot. A year after he lost the Presidency, in an interview with *Le Point*, Valéry Giscard d'Estaing, attributed his downfall at the polls in large part to the "Jewish issue."

According to a public opinion survey released on October 11, 1980, 55% of those interviewed thought that anti-Semitism was either "very" or "sufficiently" widespread. A year earlier, a social psychologist analyzing the results of another survey concluded that, "anti-Jewish feeling does not have to be overtly expressed for its presence to be confirmed."[22] Emeric Deutsch pointed out that when 17% of the population declare that they have nothing against Jews, but that there are "too many of them," they reveal a sentiment similar to someone announcing: "I am not a racist, but I am against my country being invaded by strangers." Deutsch observed that such a "mechanism consists of displacing drives that are difficult to express directly. It illustrates well the fact that racial hatred has more than one trick in its bag."[23] The rise of xenophobia, from 51% in 1968 to 61% in 1977, did not imply a lessening of anti-Jewish sentiment. The fact that there was an increase of hostility against foreigners, particularly North African Arabs, was no consolation to French Jews. Moreover, the implications of another survey on the strength of anti-Semitism in France, the results of which were never released, strongly suggested that ther were few signs of its ebbing.

In the spring of 1982, shortly before the outbreak of the war in Lebanon, an eminent French sociologist completed an extensive survey on anti-Semitism in France that was commissioned by a major Jewish community organization. The results of the in-depth survey, based on lengthy interviews of individuals and small groups in Paris as well as in other regions of France, were so distressing that the executive committee of the organization decided not to make it public. The study showed that virtually the whole anti-Semitic mythology that has been prevalent in France since the last part of the nineteenth century was still alive.[24]

Most of the individuals interviewed — included among them were both men and women, workers, and members of liberal professions of different age groups — held views that ranged over the entire spectrum of anti-Semitica. Most believed in such hardcore anti-Semitic canards as that Jews bring malediction wherever they live, think only of money, and would go to any lengths to obtain it. Jews control banks and "international capitalism." They dominate the media and show-business, which they manage to infiltrate "surreptitiously." They do not like to share power with non-Jews, do not respect conventions and traditional privileges, transgress unwritten rules in commerce and the professions, and are generally "trouble makers" who disrupt the smooth functioning of society. The interviewees also thought that the "Jewish system" is to invade a branch of commerce, to occupy it and to exclude others from it. The author of the unpublished survey pointed out that these views echoed World War II Nazi propaganda which warned of the danger of penetration of gentile society by "Jewish vermin" through a kind of microbial infection.

Participants in the survey also believed that through their educational methods Jews create elites that are capable of seizing power. Jews are inordinately intelligent and have a particular gift for handling numbers and business transactions. They are aided in this by a powerful will to success and domination. By maintaining "separatist" customs Jews threaten the foundations of French national culture. They dispossess other Frenchmen of their authentic heritage and national roots. The Jews are a closed racist group that resists penetration; yet, they manage to infiltrate non-Jewish circles when it suits their purpose.

The existence of the State of Israel has further exacerbated these anti-Semitic sentiments. Many of the accusations levelled at Jews were projected onto the Jewish state: irritation, guilt, anxiety, rivalry, strangeness as well as grudging admiration. The fear of Jews has acquired a new dimension: the Israelis are provoking trouble in the Middle East, thereby sparking the possibility of a global conflict. They are troublesome, dangerous and serve as destabilizing agents in the region. Moreover, French society is threatened by pro-Israeli French Jews whose allegiance to their country is questionable. The members of the survey group blurred distinctions between Jews and Israelis, in part because of the similarity of the terms "Israélite" (Jew) and "Israélien" (Israeli). (This ambiguity is complicated by the fact that the more common term for Jew, "Juif," preferred by the young generation, still carries strong pejorative connotations).

Although other surveys showed that there appeared to be a regression from openly declared anti-Semitism, especially among the more cultured strata of society, as well as a lessening of religiously-motivated antagonism, the in-depth survey indicated that popular Jew-hatred is still strong, particularly among women. According to the author of the survey, French anti-Semitism is characterized by its latency; relatively minor factors could bring it to the surface. Among those interviewed there was unanimous agreement that the return of open, mass anti-Semitism is almost inevitable, and that this would "cause problems" for everyone. A few months after the completion of the survey, the 1982 war in Lebanon confirmed some of its findings.

The election of François Mitterrand to the presidency in May, 1981, led many in the Jewish community to believe that a new era had dawned for the troubled relationship between France and its Jewish citizens. Mitterrand had established a reputation as a friend of Jews and of the State of Israel. His new government included several Jews (Robert Badinter, Minister of Justice, Pierre Dreyfus, Minister of Industry, Jack Lang, Minister of Culture[25]) and he appointed a man known for his activism in the Jewish community, Jacques Attali, as personal advisor.

Embittered feelings generated by repeated manifestations of verbal and physical anti-Semitism and frequent confrontations over Middle Eastern policy gave way, among Jews, to a new feeling of legitimacy, of being part of the new establishment as Frenchmen with a recognized, rightful concern for the safety of a reborn ancestral homeland. For the first time Jews began to feel that their devotion to Israel was not likely to bring accusations of double loyalty. The new administration also took concrete measures that were viewed favorably in the Jewish community. It promptly abrogated the so-called "Barre Decree," which allowed French firms to co-operate with the Arab economic boycott of Israel, and declared that the Palestine Liberation Organization was not the sole representative of the Palestinian people.

The prospects for more harmonious relations between the Jewish community and the Government and for a disappearance of the renewed manifestations of anti-Semitism were shattered, however, by reactions in the French media, and in government circles, to Israel's military action against the P.L.O. in Lebanon, in the summer of 1982. Anti-Semitism, not merely anti-Zionism, again surfaced as a serious concern.

The anti-Semitic overtones of the media coverage of the war in Lebanon were blatant, and went beyond the type of criticism normally used to show disapproval of policies of a foreign state. The virulent tone of commentators in the allegedly anti-racist left-wing press was striking. On the three Government-controlled television networks, and on the state-run radio stations, Israeli soldiers were compared to wanton Nazi troopers. French Jews were designated as accomplices and were held responsible for the military decisions of Israel's government. The media supplied to an apparently receptive public a demonic image of the Jew. The word "Zionist" became synonymous with monster, ruthless killer, Hitlerite, "the disinformation was constant."[26] In the words of a political philosopher, the media presented "into the eyes of public opinion a new image of the Jew, not of the Israeli, dressed up henceforth in the garb of those who had been [the Jews'] executioners . . . a major debate over the nature of Judaism was inaugurated."[27]

It became more evident than ever that the primary source of the new anti-Semitism was the left, which transferred some of its propaganda-laden terminology to the Jewish state as well as to Diaspora Jewry. Since the 1960s, radical factions of the French left had viewed the Middle East conflict through their "anti-imperialist" perspective. The accumulation of stereotypes that equated Zionism with American imperialism and South African racism prepared the outbursts of virulent rhetoric in the summer of 1982. In August, 1982, a prominent French-Jewish thinker wrote in reference to the leftist press: "the hysteria on the part of a great many journalists . . . was inexcusable and scandalous . . . a free press...demonstrated that it was as vulnerable to totalitarian rhetoric as a censured press."[28]

Ideologies and rhetoric that seemed to be on their way out came back to life, found a new justification for their existence in the vilification of a new "imperialism": "Sovietism may well be discredited in France, yet all factions of the left (third-worldists, pacifists, the moderates, and the anti-totalitarians), participate more or less in a myth that portrays Israel as the only state that flaunts international law."[29] In view of the large combined circulation of newspapers that espouse in various degrees left-wing thinking (Libération, Le Matin, Le Monde, L'Humanité), the impact of anti-Zionism was considerable: "a very significant slippage has taken place in the left-wing press, which no doubt influenced public opinion."[30] A well-known writer stated flatly: the hostility to Jews and Israel demonstrated a return of left-wing anti-Semitism.[31]

The philosopher, Vladimir Jankélévitch, who in the first days of the war in Lebanon joined a protest demonstration in front of the Israeli Embassy in Paris, became a few weeks later highly critical of the press coverage of the war. Jankélévitch denounced the bias and unfairness of newspapers that were generally considered moderate and respectable. He singled out *Le Monde* which, until recently, had been viewed as a compendium of French wisdom. *Le Monde*, whose hostility to the state of Israel was long-standing, presented in its editorials a demonic image of Israel's government.[32] The Paris daily editorialized that Begin's "infernal logic" leads to the "odious" and that his "infernal machine is becoming insane."[33] Jankélévitch castigated *Le Monde*'s "sophisms" and "bad faith" and accused it outright of anti-Semitism: "thus, the French have returned to their old demons. They have not been cured of the evil of anti-Semitism, or only partially."[34]

A full-page advertisement in *Le Monde* (June 17, 1982), contained open racist remarks about Jews and Judaism. The statement entitled "The Meaning of the Israeli Agression," went beyond the usual criticism of the State of Israel to accuse Jews of racism, of constituting a world-wide conspiracy ("the extraordinary hegemony of the Zionist lobby over all the media in the world") and reduced Judaism to tribalism. Signed by three personalities, Roger Garaudy, a left-wing Catholic thinker who had converted to Islam, an ardently pro-Palestinian Catholic priest, Father Michel Lelong, and Pastor Etienne Mathiot, a Protestant theologian, it referred to race and blood and distorted the meaning of Jewish identity and the concept of Jewish nationhood. Implicitly, it also called into question the Vatican II declarations on the Jews. *Le Monde* was subsequently sued for racial defamation over this advertisement by the LICRA ("Ligue Internationale Contre le Racisme et l'Antisémitisme"). The secretary of the International Federation of Human Rights told the court that the statement "recalled the 'Protocols of the Elders of Zion'."[35] *Le Monde* was eventually acquitted on the basis of a technicality.

Even left-wing academics considered the slanderous text not just "anti-Zionist, but anti-Jewish."[36] Others deplored the total silence of Church authorities who failed to denounce the anti-Semitic outbursts. For, in addition to the *Le Monde* statement such Christian publications as *Témoignage Chrétien* compared the siege of Beirut to the destruction of the Warsaw ghetto. In the third week of the war this left-wing Catholic weekly put on its cover a picture of ruins in Beirut with the caption: "The Palestinians in Beirut are like the Jews in the Warsaw Ghetto" (June 21, 1982). Georges Casalis wrote in the same publication: "The government of Jerusalem speaks of the 'final liquidation' of the Palestinians." (August 16, 1982). The widely-circulated Catholic newspaper, La Croix, also printed articles that smacked of anti-Semitism.

The silence on the part of the traditionally liberal, Catholic intellectual circles in the face of these manifestations of anti-Semitism was noted by a sociologist who wrote that "the lack of reaction on the part of the Christians was a significant . . . extremely disturbing fact, especially the lack of reaction on the part of those [liberal] Christians from whom one expected something. . . ."[37] Not unexpectedly, left-wing anti-Zionist Catholics became more influential, and more vociferous, in the summer of 1982. Some scholars, who had not been sensitized to Jewish concerns, seemed to be surprised that "the input of Christian anti-Semitism is still quite important,"[38] and that the war in Lebanon revealed "this massive phenomenon of a return of certain anti-Semitic clichés in regard to Israel and 'international Zionism'."[39]

The Communist daily, L'Humanité, waged a veritable propaganda assault on Israel. Toward the end of the war it editorialized that, "the massacre of the innocents ordered by Herod appears as a very limited crime in comparison with the murderous operations launched by Israel."[40] On the sixth day of the war, L'Humanité was already protesting "against the genocide Israel is committing in Lebanon."[41] Although the French Communist Party had lost most of its former strength L'Humanité still had a large readership and indirectly influenced other left-wing news media.[42]

Faced with this unprecedented barrage many French Jews, even those on the left who had publicly condemned the action in Lebanon, realized that their criticism was being exploited for aims that were at least in part anti-Semitic. Vladimir Jankélévitch regretted participating in the demonstration in front of the Israeli Embassy. According to the editor of a well-known weekly, French Jews had the feeling that the media took special pleasure in vilifying them and the Jewish state and that editors allowed their journalists to indulge in excessive language because they believed that they were reflecting popular sentiment.[43] Alain Finkielkraut confirmed this impression: the war in Lebanon, he wrote, "lifted a taboo that hung over anti-Semitism since Auschwitz. What abundance of benefits for the European conscience in this symbolic substitution! What happiness! What 'Schadenfreude'! What obvious relief one finds in the self-satisfaction of drawing analogies between the Star of David and the swastika."[44]

Added to what many referred to as "media bludgeoning" of the Jews were such unprecedented actions as a strike by leftist high school teachers in Paris and other cities, who demanded that France break diplomatic relations with Israel, and indoctrinated their students with anti-Zionist propaganda. The almost weekly street demonstrations organized by the Communists, leftist unions and pro-Palestinian organizations reinforced the feeling of anger and fear. According to a leader of the Jewish community "many Jews felt threatened."[45] The President of France himself appeared to have absorbed the anti-Israeli propaganda in the media when, early in July 1982, in response to a journalist's question, he seemed to agree that the bombardment of Beirut was comparable to the Nazi obliteration of a French village, Oradour-sur-Glane. Subsequent explanations that his remarks were taken out of context did not allay the feeling of gloom and dejection in the Jewish community.

When on August 9, 1982, a terrorist attack on a Jewish restaurant in the old Jewish section of Paris left six dead and twenty-two wounded it was widely believed in the Jewish community that the killers, who may have come from the Middle East, took advantage of an atmosphere filled with anti-Jewish animosity. After the murders at Goldenberg's delicatessen, some members of the media appeared to have realized that their excessive rhetoric in covering the war may have indirectly encouraged the terrorists. Soon after the rue des Rosiers shooting, Le Monde's editor wondered "if journalists ought to report the events with as much passion as was displayed by the actors of the drama in Beirut or in Paris?"[46]

The wave of hostility during the war, followed by the murders, left the Jewish community horror-stricken. Places where Jews used to gather were deserted. For weeks Jewish restaurants in Paris were almost empty of customers. In September, High Holiday attendance at synagogue services diminished noticeably, and those who had the courage to come were advised to disperse discreetly. Jewish communal centers also saw a drop in participation in their activities. The chief Rabbi of France, René Sirat, exclaimed: "once again we are alone."[47] A leader of the community expressed a widespread feeling that a pattern of violence had been set: "we wonder when the next terrorist attack will take place...knowing that it will."[48] A writer referred to the memories evoked by the new atmosphere of anxiety as "our new yellow star."[49]

Those Jews who had come to believe that their status was no longer different from that of their non-Jewish fellow countrymen began to doubt the validity of their assumptions. A community spokesman wondered if the repetition of anti-Jewish attacks in France did not create the risk of a "ghettoisation" and a "marginalisation" of Jews.[50] A prominent historian asked pointedly: "will the Jewish community... feeling rejected, cast away the existential links that tie it to France?"[51] The fact that such a split already existed, at least in some segments of the community, was expressed by a young Jewish woman interviewed by an American reporter: "I used to be completely integrated into French society... now I dissociate myself totally from the French people."[52]

Following the attack on Goldenberg's restaurant, the Israeli Prime Minister called on young French Jews to protect themselves. President Mitterrand considered this appeal an affront to France and to his own record on Jewish issues. He took stringent security measures that drastically reduced the number of anti-Jewish acts of violence. His more even-handed policies on the Middle East and gestures to improve the diplomatic climate between France and the Jewish State contributed to the relaxation of tensions. In a country where even independent newspapers are influenced by the foreign policy line emanating from the Presidential palace, there were signs that some important opinion-makers in the media were adopting a more balanced stance toward Israel. However, those on the left who considered the Palestinian issue an integral part of their ideological commitment to the Third World, the left-wing Catholics, the CERES faction of the Socialist Party, the Communist-led labour unions as well as the Communist Party itself, kept Zionist and Jewish issues in the public limelight. The politicization of the Jewish phenomenon in France had become a permanent fact.

The discussion of the role of the press in the events involving the French Jewish community, and in particular the criticisms levelled against some segments of the media during the 1982 war in Lebanon, focused attention on a world-famous daily, *Le Monde*, long considered not only the best newspaper in France, but also an untouchable institution, became the target of unprecedented criticism for its handling of the Middle East conflict and its attitude to Jews.

# Notes

[1] *L'Express*, March 20-26, 1978, pp. 105-106.

[2] Elisabeth Gille, *Le Monde*, April 18, 1979.

[3] Trigano, *La République et les Juifs*, p. 18.

[4] S. Joly, *Libération*, Oct. 6, 1980.

[5] Daniel Mayer in *L'Arche* (November, 1980), p. 32.

[6] G. Kiejman, *Le Monde*, Oct. 7, 1980.

[7] J. Bialot, *Libération*, Oct. 6, 1980.

[8] *Libération*, Oct. 6, 1980.

[9] *Ibid.*

[10] "Des adolescents jugent," *Le Journal des communautés* (November, 1980).

[11] *Le Monde*, Oct. 5-6, 1980. In February, 1977, Abou Daoud, the alleged mastermind of the murder of Israeli athletes at the Munich Olympics, was released after being arrested by French police acting on an Interpol warrant. In March, 1979 a bomb injured 30 Jewish students in a Paris restaurant. A fifteen year-old boy from Paris was killed in a P.L.O. attack against a group of Jewish children in Antwerp, in July, 1980.

[12] *Le Quotidien de Paris*, Oct. 6, 1980.

[13] *Le Monde*, Oct. 12-13, 1980.

[14] Trigano, *La République et les Juifs*, p. 24.

[15] *Le Monde*, Oct. 9, 1980.

[16] *Ibid.*

[17] *L'Arche* (November, 1980) p. 32.

[18] A point argued by Annie Kriegel in *The New York Times Magazine*, Nov. 30, 1980.

[19] The *Times* of London noted that while anti-Semitic incidents had taken place elsewhere in Europe, they did not reach the same degree of intensity as in France (Oct. 6, 1980).

[20] G. Ribière, *Information juive* (October, 1980).

[21] *Nous autres Juifs*, p. 70.

[22] Emeric Deutsch, "Les Français sont-ils antisémites?," *L'Arche* (Sept.-Oct. 1979), p. 66.

[23] *Ibid.*

[24] The author was allowed to see the survey shortly upon its completion, in May, 1982.

[25] Although not chosen directly by Mitterrand, one of the leading figures of the French Communist Party, Charles Fitterman, who became Minister of Transport, was also of Jewish origin.

[26] Alain Finkielkraut, quoted in G. Walker, "Divided They Stand," *The B'nai Brith International Jewish Monthly* (March, 1983), p. 8.

[27] B. Barret-Kriegel in "Dérapage de la gauche?," *Les Nouveaux cahiers*, no. 71 (Winter, 1982-83), p. 10.

[28] A. Finkielkraut, *La Réprobation d'Israël* (Paris: Denoël-Gonthier, 1983), p. 132.

[29]*Ibid.*, p. 121.

[30]B. Barret-Kriegel, *Les Nouveaux cahiers*, no. 71, p. 10.

[31]B.-H. Lévy, *Le Monde*, Sept. 9, 1982.

[32]On *Le Monde's* inimical attitude toward Israel, see Chapter V.

[33]*Le Monde*, July 29, 1982.

[34]*Traces*, no. 5 (Automne, 1982), p. 27.

[35]*Le Monde*, March 19, 1983.

[36]B. Barret-Kriegel, *Les Nouveaux cahiers*, no. 71, p. 13.

[37]D. Lindenberg in "Dérapage de la gauche?," *Les Nouveaux cahiers*, no. 71, p. 15.

[38]P.-A. Taguieff in "Dérapage de la gauche?," *Les Nouveaux cahiers*, no. 71, p. 12.

[39]*Ibid.*, p. 13.

[40]August 4, 1982.

[41]June 12, 1982, quoted in Annie Kriegel, *Israël est-il coupable?* (Paris: Laffont, 1982), p. 53.

[42]*Ibid.*, pp. 56-57.

[43]Richard Liscia, editor of *Les Nouvelles littéraires*, interviewed on May 11, 1983.

[44]Finkielkraut, *La Réprobation d'Israël*, p. 57.

[45]Henri Hajdenberg, the leader of "Renouveau Juif," in a conversation with the author on May 6, 1983.

[46]Aug. 11, 1982.

[47]Quoted in G. Walker, "Divided They Stand," *B'nai Brith International*, p. 8.

[48]H. Hajdenberg, quoted in *Le Monde*, Sept. 24, 1982.

[49]I. Starkier, in *Le Monde*, Sept. 25, 1982.

[50]Emile Touati in an interview on Israel Radio French Language Service, October 5, 1982.

[51]Emmanuel Le Roy Ladurie in "Dérapage de la gauche?," *Les Nouveaux cahiers*, no. 71, p. 18.

[52]Quoted in Walker, *B'nai Brith International*, p. 13.

# CHAPTER V
# Le Monde

The ability to inform is also the ability to exercise power. In the modern history of journalism in Western, democratic countries, few newspapers have possessed as much influence and power as the Paris daily, *Le Monde*. In four decades it has managed to establish such a hold on French social and political life that even the highest echelons of the political establishment took into account its opinons and judgments. Required daily reading for the country's large intelligentsia as well as for those governing France, *Le Monde* became a force whose "slightest opinons have acquired considerable, at times exorbitant authority."[1] Moreover, *Le Monde's* "prestige, power and prosperity" seemed to protect it from its detractors.[2]

In no other Western democracy has one newspaper succeeded in monopolizing to such a great extent the authority over both moral and cultural standards. *Le Monde* became "the *compendium* of French culture, the monitor of the intelligentsia and of French politics" to a point that "nothing really counts if it had not appeared in it."[3] Not surprisingly, *Le Monde* has come to view itself as the "conscience of France."[4] In addition, because of its large foreign sales its impact on the world's intelligentsia is far from negligible.[5]

The power of the "indispensible" Paris newspaper became so awesome that even sympathetic critics refrained from exceeding certain limits, because *Le Monde* induced "a kind of fear."[6] Due to its reputation for independence, promptness in supplying its readers with specialized analyses of both foreign and domestic events, and because its high technical and linguistic standard, *Le Monde* became an institution whose influence was immense. A power struggle over a successor to its retiring editor was watched with great interest by the "Presidential palace, the French foreign office, as well as by foreign embassies."[7] By virtue of the fact that the French daily press is generally of a low caliber *Le Monde* enjoys "a virtual monopoly of serious readership and has no real rival in sight."[8] With its 600,000 circulation *Le Monde* had, in proportionate terms, twice as many readers as *The New York Times*. Yet, paradoxically, its role in French life has "barely been studied."[9]

The attitudes expressed in this powerful newspaper toward French Jewry provided a significant barometer of anti-Jewish sentiment in France. The appearance in May, 1980 of a virulent attack on the integrity and loyalty of French Jewry, replete with anti-Semitic clichés, was above all indicative of the level anti-Jewish discourse had reached in *Le Monde*. The threats and accusations of double loyalty came from the pen of a professor of history whose views *Le Monde* considered worthy of being printed on the page it devotes to the opinions of experts.

Entitled "Double Nationality, Double Allegiance,"[10] the article by Professor M.L. Snoussi openly levelled the charge of treason against French Jewry. It contained one of the most explicit formulations in the mass media of the post-Holocaust period of a nineteenth-century anti-Semitic cliché: Jews are "cosmopolitans," foreigners, who use countries like France as a temporary base for exploiting the non-Jewish population. The article called for a "clarification" of the status of Jews in France or "in any other country."

The history professor linked the charge of cosmopolitanism to a new element in the old "Jewish domination" theory, the modern State of Israel. French Jewry — Snoussi interchangeably referred to it as "the Jews of France" or as "the Jewish Zionists of France" — was also suspected of setting bombs to injure fellow Jews, of seizing control of the French media, of forming powerful lobbies, of Machiavellian behavior and of intimidating and insulting the President of France. Thinly-veiled threats accompanied this diatribe.

The article, prefaced by the editors of *Le Monde* as a reaction to the "problem of double allegiance," contained phrases which in other democratic countries would be considered as incitement to racial violence: "In fact, who do they [the French Jews] belong to? What is their true nationality? To which government do they owe their allegiance?...Isn't this double allegiance, especially if it involves a foreign state, a form of 'treason'?" The French Jews, falsely described by Snoussi as "immigrants" (read "foreigners"), spread confusion "through their seizure of the mass media." Their "insolence" and "intimidation" creates pressure through strong lobbies "similar to those of New York Jews." The article included a warning against Jewish attempts to persuade the government to change its Middle East policy: "The unwarranted interference by French Zionists in French foreign policy, a policy supported by most Frenchmen, can only do harm to the Jews themselves, because their attitudes exasperate the majority of Frenchmen...."

"France must be full of traitors," commented the author of an article criticizing Snoussi in the intellectual monthly, *Les Temps Modernes*. The "traitors" are not only Zionists but Catholics loyal to the Vatican, Maoists linked to China, Moscow loyalists, those who oppose French intervention in Chad, and many others in disagreement with the policies of the administration in power. But, the caustic *Temps Modernes* writer added, "Jews are different, they are not French."[11] The Snoussi article encouraged chauvinism "by presenting the Jews as second class citizens...whose pedigree leaves something to be desired and who plot with a foreign power."[12] Another writer in the same monthly thought that "he was dreaming" when he saw this article published "by a great left-wing liberal newspaper...only forty years after the Nazi extermination camps." The content of the Snoussi article reminded him of anti-Semitic, Vichy rhetoric, of "the French suppliers of death camps."[13]

Professor Snoussi also wrote that since the first Zionist Congress in Basel, in 1897, Jews have adopted an attitude of dual allegiance, and since 1948 they have limited their loyalty to one entity: Israel. The author of the *Le Monde* article was not content to question the Jews' loyalty to France; he also suggested that in order to stimulate immigration "to Palestine," Zionists deliberately provoke anti-Semitism and "encourage such acts" as the March, 1979 bombing of a Jewish student restaurant in Paris. The publication of this article in the pages of the most influential French daily was an indication of a dangerous loosening of constraints on the use of anti-Semitic rhetoric.

In a letter to the editor a member of the Jewish community exclaimed : "Some of us, French Jews, are beginning to have our fill of newspaper articles on Jews. For goodness' sake, forget about us for a while!"[14] He also charged that "without any question" the Snoussi outburst was woven from "a fabric of anti-Semitic slanders that you [*Le Monde*] publish without any corrective or reproving note." Referring to the erroneous Snoussi statement that the majority of French Jews were immigrants, the French-born surgeon asked: "For how many generations will my family be considered as immigrants? You are reminding me of the [racist] Vichy legislation that I have forgotten." The reader went on to accuse *Le Monde*, "the newspaper of the French intelligentsia," of printing an article which would have "delighted" the editors of the anti-Semitic *Je Suis Partout*, published in the 1940s. He added that he intends to bring up his children to be mistrustful, and that he will tell them that people sharing the mentality of the French Gendarmes, who during the war "took him away to be assassinated," are still "ensconced even in newspapers pretending to be highly respectable."

In the same issue, an official of a Jewish organization accused *Le Monde* of "shedding all restraints," and asked how it could have printed such a "hateful and gratuitous pamphlet of rare violence."[15] The historical errors and the distorted quotations alone, André Wurmser wrote, "should have forbidden the publication of this text." He also expressed his indignation about this "truly infamous aggression against an authentic part of the French nation." When "the leaders of the community are pictured as assassins of their own children," Wurmser continued, "odiousness reaches its peak." Strangely, the newspaper that has been outspoken in condemning racism around the world provided a forum for a French racist.

Following the rue Copernic explosion, it seemed for a while that attacks on French Jewry in the Paris daily had come to an end. However, barely three months after the bombing, another spurt of anti-Semitic verbiage appeared in *Le Monde*. In early January, 1981, on its front page this time, it published an article entitled "A Letter to my Jewish Friends," by a man identified as a writer.[16] The unusually lengthy article marked a further escalation in *Le Monde's* permissiveness on the expression of anti-Jewish discourse. Under the guise of "friendly advice" from a "goy" (as the author referred to himself) who supposedly admires Judaism, Jean-Marie Paupert managed to incorporate some of the crudest classical accusations against Jews into a diatribe worded in a way to inflict the deepest insult. The article also included offensive remarks against the most respected Jewish political figure in France, Simone Veil.

French Jews who protest anti-Semitism in their country must be driven by some "sadistic devil," writes Paupert. "Inside you [Jews]," he continues, "hides a malicious, masochistic spirit that wants...to prove that there exists anti-Semitic venom in France, for the sole purpose of enabling you to feel woeful, to be able to weep and to demand justice and forgiveness." In a clear reference to the debate in the press on Vichy's treatment of Jews and on the Holocaust J.-M. Paupert asks: "when will you stop demanding that we come to ask you to forgive us for Hitler's crimes wearing a shirt, a rope around our necks, and holding a candle in our hands?"

How dare the Jews claim to be victims of discrimination when it is, on the contrary, he, the Frenchman, who is the victim of Jewish aggression: "they have been too numerous, of late, those who spend themselves in insult, aggression and threats against anyone hastily suspected of anti-Semitic intentions." He warns that he is not "one to tolerate such treatment." By protesting too loudly the attacks against them the Jews "rekindle the exasperation" even of the most good-natured Frenchmen. (The verb "exaspérer" is repeated several times: "You exasperate the population [of France]," "a problem that...exasperates the people"). It is, writes Paupert, the "excessive reaction," the "noise" raised by Jews in the media and on the street, that has contributed to the bombing of the rue Copernic synagogue. The Jews, he suggests, should behave with "greater humility."

The author of the Le Monde article asked Jews to learn how to keep quiet, to know their place. Above all, they must not complain, for their plight is not unique: "it is one of your irritating manias to think that you were the only persecuted people in the world, and the one to suffer the greatest persecutions." Unless they learn better ways, Jews risk retribution: "by crying wolf, you should fear provoking the beast that could emerge some horrible night from the shady bush." Jews should know that it is "imprudent" to suspect and to insult the French people. This was one of several intimations in the article that the Jews are not part of the French people.

After the rue Copernic explosion Jews obtained what they wanted, Paupert continued: "contrite saliva, sticky ink, tearjerking prose and even some holy water." Simone Veil's concerns about the proliferation of neo-Nazi rhetoric he termed "whining, incoherent babbling." The article was also replete with anti-Semitic clichés and insults. The Jews "are swift to adapt themselves to situations," are "sharp analysts" and "astute investors" (in classical anti-Semitic literature they were denoted as "cosmopolitans and clever manipulators"). Jews are "by nature" rebellious. Their "contesting virus" has led them to cooperate with the

Russian revolutionaries. Simone Veil, who as Minister of Health championed an abortion law, is a criminal whose hand Paupert would refuse to shake.

The Paupert article also contained the inevitable charge of double loyalty. The accusations were couched in particularly offensive terminology. Jews "don't know what they want or who they are," their identity is expressed in terms of "maybe yes, maybe no." Mimicking a French Jew Paupert writes: "Am I a Jew? Sh ... don't be a racist, I am a Frenchman, Sir, maybe more than you, for several generations; my father fought at Verdun and my grandfather died in a charge at Reichshoffen." Racism was also implicit in comments aimed to prove the author's "friendship" to Jews: his children, he wrote to prove that he is a Judeophile, are "quadroons" and his grandchildren "octavons," and the region where he was born was "always fertile in Jewish communities."

If Le Monde's previous articles hostile to Jews went generally unanswered by the Parisian intelligentsia, this time there was a loud response. In an eloquent denunciation of Paupert, Olivier Todd, then editor of L'Express, commented on the insult to Simone Veil. "Paupert proclaims that he would refuse to shake Simone Veil's hand! Does he fear to become soiled? Simone Veil and the abortion law personify, in 1981, the Jew who kills Christian children."[17]

"Lettre à mes amis juifs" also drew a sharp response in the weekly Le Nouvel Observateur, which agrees with Le Monde on most issues. It gave prominent space to Simone de Beauvoir who demanded that Le Monde repudiate the content of its article, which she termed a "foul spurt" of anti-Semitism and a "diatribe inspired by Drumont."[18] Sartre's life-long companion wrote that "never before was racism so impudently displayed" in the newspaper which she "long suspected of hidden prejudice." Freedom of expression cannot be at issue since "insults can in no manner constitute information." Paupert should have published his article in "some racist sheet." Simone de Beauvoir also wondered why the unknown Paupert ranks so highly to earn the privilege of being published on page one of Le Monde, when the editors of the daily "do not hesitate to refuse articles that do not suit them."

To show its "fairness" Le Monde published two rebuttals to the Paupert article.[19] The bland and apologetic response by Rabbi Josy Eisenberg failed to express the indignation felt by many Jews. The much sharper reply by a Christian philosopher, concerned over the harm Paupert may have caused to Jewish-Christian dialogue, was unequivocal in its disapproval. Jean-Marie Benoist denounced the "inadmissable cheekiness which pretends to be ignorant of history," and the attempt to convince the French that "if the Jews were persecuted from generation to generation it is evidently because of their guilt."[20] The fact that Le Monde allowed only two rebuttals was an indication of its desire to quash the controversy.[21] Awarding equal space to the anti-Semite and to his critics amounted to placing both arguments on the same level. It was a reflection of a Le Monde practice "of legitimizing both and conferring on them the same respectability."[22]

Olivier Todd's article skillfully pinpointed the many malicious insinuations in "a text which oozes with anti-Semitism."[23] The one-time protegé of Jean-Paul Sartre asked the question that should have been raised several years earlier: "What ever is happening in France today? . . . how could they print a repugnant anti-Semitic collection of insults on page one of Le Monde?" Todd expressed his indignation that Paupert dared to revive the image of the money-hungry Jew, which he (Todd) has "not seen displayed so prominently since the days of the German occupation."

Referring to the cliché evoked by such terms as "contrite saliva," the prominent journalist wrote: "The image of the Jew driveling at the mouth reminds me of the German Propagandastaffel posters on the walls of Paris in 1943." Alluding to Paupert's charge of double loyalty against French Jewry, Todd commented: "forty years ago the Jews were presented [by the Nazis] as the Trojan horse of the United States or of England. Today some individuals see them performing a similar mission for Israel." He further accused Le Monde of offering a forum to "old, militant anti-Semitic themes, clichés and myths." The article also deplored the passive response to the Paupert diatribe of France's chief Rabbi, René Sirat, who had refused to comment on it during a television interview. A few months later Todd denounced the editors of Le Monde for presenting anti-Semitism as "just another [legitimate] opinion among others."[24]

This denunciation of verbal anti-Semitism by some of France's most prominent intellectual and media figures was a rare, long-overdue call for a stop to an ugly campaign. De Beauvoir's and Todd's reactions were echoed by other well-known intellectuals. The philosopher, Vladimir Jankélévitch, characterized Paupert's article as "revolting hypocrisy." He added that he was "scandalized that Le Monde would devote such prominent space to mediocre prose."[25] Phillipe Sollers, the editor of the intellectual quarterly,

*Tel quel*, was also shocked by "the stupidity and vulgarity of a text" that belonged "to old anti-Semitic lore."[26] For a journal published by a prominent civil rights organization *Le Monde* "made respectable ideas that are not merely opinions but constitute a provocation which assaults dignity...."[27] B.-H. Lévy considered the article as a "catalogue of the most classical kind of anti-Semitism" and pointed the finger at those responsible for printing it: "the real scandal...is that when, unsuspecting, I buy *Le Monde* to read the news I get this aggressive act flung in my face."[28]

The debate over the Paupert article also brought out the fact that those who condoned the open publication of anti-Semitic material did not constitute an isolated minority. The liberal journalist, Dominique Jamet, criticized Simone de Beauvoir for denouncing Paupert "merely because he dared to pronounce opinions different from hers," and characterized her views as "intellectual terrorism."[29] A writer in the popular weekly, *Nouvelles littéraires*, also attacked de Beauvoir for her "intellectual counterterrorism."[30] Louis Pauwels, the editor of *Figaro-Magazine*, and a leader of the "New Right," thought that Paupert's article "placed the debate [on the Jews] on a high level of reflection and dignity," and that such a debate is "legitimate and useful."[31] Paupert himself claimed that he received many expressions of thanks for the courage "to say things no one had dared to express before."[32] Mocking those who objected to the Paupert diatribe, a writer in an intellectual Catholic monthly remarked sarcastically: "the subject is taboo, the Jews have the privileges of untouchables. To speak about them is to commit an impropriety and to trigger a bad conscience."[33]

"As we all know, *Le Monde* has never felt a great deal of passion for the State of Israel,"[34] writes the author of an admiring book on *Le Monde*. A critic of *Le Monde*, with an intimate knowledge of its ideology and operations, was more outspoken in characterizing *Le Monde*'s coverage of the Arab-Israeli conflict as being "almost always in Israel's disfavour."[35] Even before the sharp turn in France's Middle Eastern policy in 1967, *Le Monde*'s hostility to the State of Israel was noted by a French political scientist. In a survey of the French press in 1958, J.W. Lapierre noted a sharp contrast between *Le Monde*'s coverage of Israel and that of other dailies. He found that only two newspapers, the Communist *L'Humanité* and the extreme-left *Libération*, carried a larger number of unfavorable stories on Israel.[36] Since 1967, *Le Monde* has been generally favorable to the Arab cause and has displayed "systematic ill-will"[37] toward the Jewish state. The author of a University of Paris doctoral dissertation has claimed that Le Monde has a disguised anti-Israeli bias.[38] Although criticism of Israel is not necessarily an indication of anti-Jewish sentiment, a consistently hostile attitude arouses suspicion.

In general terms, Le Monde's positions on the Middle East conflict (at least until it changed editors in 1983), reflected the following line: the Arabs have been consistently moderate while Israel, whether governed by the Labour or the Likud parties, has been unyielding. The key to any peaceful solution lies in Israel's willingness to make concessions and to grant the Palestinians self-determination. At best, Israel's refusal to be conciliatory is due to an "obsession with security," at worst it represents grandiose desires for a Jewish empire and fanatical religious mysticism.[39] Israel is responsible for the tragedy of the Arab refugees and P.L.O. terrorism has to be understood in the context of the suffering experienced by the Palestinians. The Jewish state is a foreign element in the Middle East, a colonial power, brutally repressing an indigenous liberation movement.[40] Big power intervention, especially by the United States, is essential, but it is constantly thwarted by an omnipotent Jewish lobby. It is in France's long-range political, economic and strategic interest to foster close ties with the Arab world, as it is her traditional obligation to maintain historical cultural links with Islam.[41]

Critics of Le Monde have pointed out that it entrusted the coverage of the Middle East "almost exclusively to journalists of Jewish origin."[42] But in selecting them it did not overlook their political orientation, or the fact that they could serve as a convenient alibi against accusations of a pro-Arab bias. Le Monde's chief Middle Eastern editor and editorialist for two decades was a talented journalist, Eric Rouleau, the former editor of a bulletin for a Jewish fund-collecting agency, who was hired by Le Monde in 1962. This leftist Jewish intellectual, fluent in several languages, became one of the most effective apologists for the Arab cause in Europe and in North America, where he was often interviewed by the media.[43]

Le Monde's resident correspondents in the Middle East have invariably been leftists, at times of the extreme variety, who specialized in denigrating Israel's foreign and domestic policies. Thus Amnon Kapeliouk, an extreme-leftist, was for many years the interpreter of Israel's social and political scene for an influential readership in France. Kapeliouk's reportage, often a form of social commentary, concentrated primarily on stories about illegal arrests of Arabs and social injustice.[44] This pattern of coverage was in line with one of Le Monde's methods, which lends a "kind of serial dignity,"[45] to events that acquire significance through repetition. The extensive coverage of Israeli domestic issues that reflected negatively on the country's image was a practice Le Monde rarely followed in reporting on other foreign states.

For many years, Le Monde's permanent correspondent in Beirut was the editor of the French-language Lebanese daily, L'Orient-Le Jour, Edouard Saab. Saab was a staunch advocate of left-wing Arab nationalism and he held anti-Semitic views.[46] His connection with Le Monde represents perhaps one of the best illustrations of the slant in the newspaper's coverage of the Middle East. As an editor of a local newspaper, working in a city where journalists were often assassinated for displeasing extremist groups, he could hardly be expected to supply objective information. Thus, when P.L.O. terrorists blew up a Swiss airliner bound for Israel and killed forty-seven travellers, Le Monde printed a dispatch from Saab which included "the hypothesis" that the terrorist act was a "Zionist provocation" and that this view was "gaining ground."[47] Few other authoritative Western newspapers employed on a permanent basis the services of a strongly biased editor of a local daily in a strife-torn country. Saab's successor, Lucien George, also a Lebanese leftist, has been hardly more objective. He wrote matter-of-factly that the United Nations peacekeeping forces are aware of Israel's "conceit" and quickly discover its "arrogance and bad faith."[48]

Another questionable Le Monde practice involved citing Israeli sources without indicating their extreme, or unrepresentative, political viewpoint. Felicia Langer, Uri Avneri and Matityahu Peled have been among those quoted as allegedly objective spokesmen, without any mention of the fact that the first, a defense counsel for Arab extremists, is a member of the Central Committee of the Israeli Communist Party, the second a highly controversial leftist editor of a scandal-seeking magazine, and the third a sympathiser of the P.L.O. and a member of the Marxist Progressive List for Peace. In reporting on a trial of Palestinian terrorists in an Israeli court, Le Monde indentified their lawyer, Felicia Langer, the high-ranking Communist, merely as a "survivor of Polish ghettos."[49] Writing about the criticisms levelled against a general who commited blunders during the Yom Kippur War, Le Monde[50] mentioned that the Israeli press called him another Captain Dreyfus, without revealing that the "press" was, in fact, Uri Avneri's leftist scandal sheet, *Ha'olam Hazeh*. In another issue, the headline of a lengthy, prominently displayed interview with Matityahu Peled referred to him only as the former "chief of logistics of the Israeli army."[51] His Marxist, pro-P.L.O. political affiliations were not disclosed.

In addition to the slanted material supplied to it by its own correspondents, *Le Monde* often printed the views of a number of anti-Zionist and leftist French Jews who were grossly unfair in their criticism of Israel. While *Le Monde*'s editors are careful to point our that their columns are open to a variety of opinions, balanced, pro-Israeli viewpoints saw print only on rare occasions. Pierre Vidal-Naquet, an avowed anti-Zionist, Maxime Rodinson, an anti-Zionist orientalist with old ties to Communism, and Wladimir Rabi, an acerbic critic of Israel and of the French-Jewish "establishment,"[52] were among the most prominent Jewish "personalities" whose articles have appeared repeatedly in *Le Monde*. To "balance" the stance of the anti-Zionists *Le Monde* printed occasionally the right-wing views of the Jewish writer, Paul Giniewski, casting him in the role of a "typical" Zionist.

Since the 1967 shift in French policy toward Israel, *Le Monde*'s articles have contained comparisons between Israelis and Nazis, stories on Israeli atrocities, and comments condoning Arab terrorism. *Le Monde*'s hostility did not diminish even when Israel was on the brink of defeat following the surprise attack by Egypt and Syria in 1973. In the middle of the Yom Kippur War it published violently anti-Israeli articles by the P.L.O.'s Paris envoy, by a Soviet journalist ("A New Israeli Aggression"), and by an anti-Zionist French politician (Oct. 18). It also chose at the moment of Israel's near-defeat, to publish articles entitled "For the Palestinians" (Oct. 20), and "The Right of the Palestinians" (Oct. 24).

In 1974, a few months after the Yom Kippur War, *Le Monde* suggested a parallel between the destruction of the Syrian fortress town of Kuneitra during the fighting on the Golan Heights, and the obliteration by German SS troops of the French town of Oradour-sur-Glane, along with its inhabitants, in what was the single most barbaric atrocity committed by the Germans on French soil during World War II. In a series of articles and letters to the editor the newspaper conducted a veritable campaign of defamation against the Jewish state, still under the trauma of a devastating attack. "Can Kuneitra be compared to Oradour-sur-Glane?" asked the *Le Monde* writer. Although the article concluded that the parallel is unfitting (most of the civilians had been evacuated from the border town before the start of the hostilities), the insinuation was unmistakable. Even the conclusion, absolving the Israelis from a Nazi-type crime, contained a slur: "At the end of 1973 there were only a dozen inhabitants left, and from this point of view, at least, the comparison with Nazism is inappropriate."[53] The clear implication was that from other points of view the comparison was indeed valid.[54]

In 1975, following the massacre of school children in the Israeli town of Ma'alot, in an article entitled "A Heart of Stone," Le Monde seemed to be genuinely indignant about the Palestinian atrocity. Yet the condemnation was followed by a comment that tended to stifle the reader's anger against the killers: "How much resentment must have accumulated in order to change into stone the hearts of these men, many of whom have children for whose lives they tremble like all fathers!"[55] In fact, most P.L.O. suicide squads have been composed of very young males, unattached and highly indoctrinated. After another attack on Israeli school children, at Kiryat-Shmoneh, Le Monde's very reproval managed to restore the image of the terrorists, through the comment that a war waged against women and children does not "transform into heroes" those who lose their lives "courageously" in the terrorist act. Le Monde's indulgent attitude toward indiscriminate terrorism has been marked by repeated efforts to minimize its immoral dimension in the name of a "just struggle" by "frustrated," "oppressed" groups. A prominent publicist remarked that while the barbarity of terrorism may shock public opinion, "this does not prevent [Le Monde] from finding  political explanations which diminish the force of the indignation."[56]

On the Middle East conflict Le Monde has either invented its own terminology or has adopted the more valorizing terms used by Arab extremists. The P.L.O. forces in Lebanon and their allies were invariably named "Palestino-progressistes," although the politics of none of the factions in Lebanon could be termed "progressive." After the Camp David accords, the hard-line Arab states, who were referred to in the Western press as the "Rejectionist Front," became in Le Monde the "Front de la fermeté" (firmness), the appellation preferred by the Arab extremists themselves. Arab terrorism against civilians in  Israel was routinely called "la résistance palestinienne," when for most Frenchmen the term "résistance" echoes the image of the valiant partisans who fought the German occupiers in World War II. Le

*Monde* has also referred to the P.L.O. as "maquisards," an even more direct reminder of the "maquis," the French World War II guerilla fighters. Conversely, the Israelis were often called "occupants," an emotionally charged term with World War II resonances. The Israeli attempts to control blind terrorism were described as "la répression," also a word with associations to harsh German occupation practices.

Readers not thoroughly familiar with *Le Monde* may wonder about the value of efforts to detect such innuendos in a medium functioning within strict limitations of time and space. The authors of a book on *Le Monde* have addressed themselves to this question: "Why speak about what escapes a cursive reading of the newspaper? It's because we are dealing with a type of editorial comment, specific to *Le Monde*, containing a secondary level of discoure...What is not said, but suggested — either implicitly by an inaudible silence, or through oblique syntax — stimulates certain conditioned reflexes, induces certain attitudes, reinforces certain behavior, promoting or creating a state of receptivity to an ideology propagated by the newspaper, which is foisted fraudulently upon the reader's subconscious."[57]

Seemingly insignificant stylistic devices can give a story a particular twist, a single word can change the implication of a fact, and typographical signs can transform facts into opinions.[58] A box around a brief article creates greater attention and more impact than a longer story placed — supposedly for balance — on the same page. In his unpublished doctoral thesis on *Le Monde*, Lucien Klausner disclosed that in 1971, for example, the Paris daily carried ten times as many "boxed" articles — readily commanding attention and critical of Israel — than on its Arab foes. Quotation marks, italics, brief comments in parentheses and in bolder type can influence the hurried reader subconsciously. At times this latter device, never longer than a brief paragraph, can contain editorial comment intended to sway the reader's opinion about a news item or even (surprisingly, for an allegedly independent newspaper) to persuade him of the correctness of official policy![59]

From 1967 on, in its "Open Forum" and "Ideas" sections *Le Monde* has portrayed the Israelis as, among other, Roman conquerors,[60] as ambitious colonizers driven by global aspirations, and as imposters wrongfully claiming historical rights. Aroused by this persistant pattern of hostility, the eminent historian, Alain Besançon, commented that *Le Monde* "has persevered in developing through anti-Zionism a very consistent anti-Jewish policy . . . and has published highly shocking caricatures and headlines."[61]

The frequent *Le Monde* contributor, Philippe de Saint-Robert, echoed *The Protocols of the Elders of Zion*: "Israel is a purely colonial fact, the metropoli of an elusive and omnipresent empire."[62] Another regular columnist, Gabriel Matzneff, saw the Israelis as foreign invaders: "It is hard to see what authorizes the descendants of the Khazars, this Tartar nation of Southern Russia which converted to Judaism at the time of Charlemagne, to expel from Nazareth and Nablus Arab Semites who have been living there forever . . . ."[63] Still another contributor distorted facts and history matter-of-factly: "Jerusalem is mainly an Arab city."[64]

It has been pointed out that *Le Monde* uses its "Open Forum" section to expound its political and ideological orientation by printing the views of selected "experts," often intellectuals eager to be published in a highly prestigious newspaper. These intellectuals are, according to a former *Le Monde* journalist, "both alibis and hostages."[65] Jewish intellectuals, often left-wingers and militant secularists, make particularly convenient alibis. Thus *Le Monde* allowed an "anti-clerical" Jew to mock one of the oldest Jewish religious ceremonies while attacking Menahem Begin a few weeks after he was elected Prime-Minister.

In July, 1977, *Le Monde* published in its "Open Forum"[66] an article by Rabi entitled "The Suicidal Urge".[67] The author violently attacked Begin and his religious coalition partners, using language that offended religious sensitivities and echoed anti-Semitic clichés. Depicting Begin's participation in a traditional Torah dedication ceremony in a new settlement, Rabi described him carrying the Torah scroll, "bound in velvet and gold like an idol from Canaanitic times."[68] For anyone not familiar with the ceremony Rabi's comments suggested that Begin was guilty of idolatry. The juxtaposition of the words "gold" and "idol" evoked the old image of the gold-worshipping Jews. Rabi also referred to the "biological [racist] nature" of Jewish law.

To understand what motivated *Le Monde*'s attitude to Jews some have suggested that it is necessary to consider the socio-political background of the newspaper's founders and their successors. A student of French intellectual history, commenting on *Le Monde*'s publication of J.-M. Paupert's anti-Semitic diatribe, offered a partial explanation: "I believe that in *Le Monde*, as everywhere in France, one can find a weighty heritage which has been handed down through the years and which reveals symptoms of this kind.

The Paupert symptom is a perfect reflection of the continuity of the history of *Le Monde* and of French ideology. Articles like Paupert's are not meteors that simply drop from the sky."[69]

*Le Monde*'s attitude to Israel was linked to its political outlook. Its "global hypothesis" reflected the thinking of that segment of the French non-Communist left that is hostile to capitalism and to the "mercantile" United States.[70] This stance, combined with its anti-colonialism, forged in the 1950s in the struggle against the French presence in Indochina and Algeria, was transferred to the reborn Jewish state. The fact that the founders of Israel were mostly of European origin, and that they sought vital financial support from the United States, was in itself sufficient to discredit the Jewish state as an outpost of colonialism and American "imperialism."

Although he founded *Le Monde* in part "to further Catholic aims,"[71] Hubert Beuve-Méry selected a group of collaborators who were deeply committed to a left-wing, anti-colonialist and anti-American ideology. His hand-picked successor, Jacques Fauvet, nudged the political outlook of the newspaper further to the left, tirelessly promoting a variety of leftist and Third World causes, including that of the Palestinians.[72] Zionist Israel, America's "foothold" in the Middle East, stood for a triple heresy to *Le Monde*'s Catholicism, progressivism and anti-Americanism. This, combined with a general lack of sensitivity to Jewish concerns resulted in consistently unfair and excessive criticism of the Jewish state and made for the acceptance of anti-Semitic expression as a legitimate means of public debate.

# Notes

[1]J.-N. Jeanneney and J. Julliard, *"Le Monde" de Beuve-Méry ou le métier d'Alceste* (Paris: Seuil, 1979), p. 306.

[2]*Ibid.*, p. 280.

[3]J.-M. Domenach, "'Le Monde' en question," *Esprit* (April, 1976), p. 778.

[4]B.-H. Lévy, *L'Arche* (February, 1981), p. 11.

[5]In 1977 the foreign sales made up fully 19% of its circulation. See J.W. Freiberg, *The French Press, Class, State and Idelogy* (New York; Praeger, 1981), p. 96.

[6]Pierre Nora, *Le Nouvel observateur*, April 12, 1976.

[7]S. White, "The Conclave at 'Le Monde'," *The Spectator*, March 1, 1980.

[8]*Ibid.*

[9]Domenach, *Esprit* (April, 1976), p. 769. Although *Le Monde*'s circulation has been diminishing, and its influence may not be as powerful as it was a few years ago, its prestige remains higher than that of any other French daily.

[10]M.L. Snoussi, *Le Monde*, May 7, 1980.

[11]"Le Sexisme ordinaire," *Les Temps modernes*, no. 407 (June, 1980), pp. 2304-2305.

[12]*Ibid.*, p. 2307.

[13]J.-C. Margolin, "Antisémitisme d'hier et d'aujourd'hui: antisémitisme éternel?," *Les Temps modernes*, no. 410 (September, 1980), p. 432.

[14]Jean Waligora, "Oubliez-nous un peu!" *Le Monde*, May 23, 1980.

[15]André Wurmser, "Sur une calomnie," *Le Monde* , May 23, 1980.

[16]J.-M. Paupert, "Lettre à mes amis juifs," Jan. 4-5, 1981.

[17]"Le Racisme fourbe," *L'Express*, Jan. 24, 1981, p. 60.

[18]"Réponse d'une Française innocente au journal '*Le Monde*'," Jan. 12-18, 1981. De Beauvoir's original draft called for a boycott of *Le Monde*. The editor of the weekly, Jean Daniel, persuaded her to omit it from the published statement.

[19]Jan. 10, 1981.

[20]*Ibid.*

[21]The editor of *Le Monde*, Jacques Fauvet, wrote to this author, somewhat cryptically, that the Paupert article "had been delayed for several weeks and ought to have been presented in a different fashion."

[22]F. Bernard, "Le Journal *Le Monde* et ses 'amis juifs'," *Information juive* (January, 1981).

[23]*L'Express*, Jan. 24, 1981.

[24]*L'Arche*, May, 1981.

[25]*Le Quotidien de Paris*, Jan. 13, 1981.

[26]*Ibid.*

[27]"Lettre ouverte au *Monde*," *Le Droit de vie*, February, 1981.

[28]*L'Arche* (February, 1981), p. 41.

[29]*Le Quotidien de Paris*, Jan. 13, 1981.

[30]Jan. 15-22, 1981.

[31]*Le Quotidien de Paris*, Jan. 13, 1981.

[32]*Ibid.*

[33]P.D., "Français Juifs Allemands," *Esprit* (February, 1981), p. 123.

[34]J. Thibau, *"Le Monde", histoire d'un journal, un journal dans l'histoire* (Paris: J.-C. Simoën, 1978), p. 455.

[35]M. Legris, *"Le Monde" tel qu'il est* (Paris: Plon, 1976), p. 143.

[36]J.W. Lapierre, *L'information sur l'Etat d'Israël dans les grands quotidiens français en 1958* (Paris: CNRS, 1968), p. 228.

[37]Legris, *"Le Monde"*, p. 188.

[38]Lucien Klausner, whose thesis, *"Le Monde et Israël, 1967-1973,"* is being prepared for publication.

[39]Rabi's article on July 2, 1977 illustrates this point. Rabi was a frequent contributor to *Le Monde*.

[40]*Le Monde*, Nov. 11, 1974. *Le Monde* has consistently depicted the Palestinians as the persecuted Jews and the Israelis as persecutors. Eric Rouleau wrote, for example, that the "Palestinian Diaspora" says like the eternal Jew in exile in his prayer, "Next year in Jerusalem!" (Oct. 8-9, 1974).

[41]This point was stressed by the editor, Jacques Fauvet, during an interview with this writer on June 24, 1975.

[42]Legris, "*Le Monde*", p. 83.

[43]Also see Jacques Hermone's sharp criticism of Rouleau in *La Gauche, Israël et les Juifs* (Paris: La Table Ronde, 1970), pp. 226-230.

[44]Jacques Fauvet conceded to this writer that Kapeliouk's emphasis on these events resulted in some distortion, but, disingenuously disclaimed responsibility for his selection as *Le Monde*'s correspondent (interview of June 24, 1975).

[45]J.-F. Revel, *La Nouvelle censure* (Paris: Laffont, 1977), p. 69.

[46]Saab's anti-Semitism emerged fully from the pages of his own Beirut newspaper: "Rather than the apocalypse we should invoke *The Protocols of the Elders of Zion*, which may quite possibly be apocryphal, the work of some awful Nazi. But doesn't this document deal with a tentacular monster ready to do any task to assure the survival and prosperity of Zionism?" (*L'Orient-Le Jour*, Jan. 8, 1974, quoted in Jacques Givet, *Israël et le génocide inachevé*, Paris: Plon, 1979, p. 113).

[47]*Le Monde*, Feb. 27, 1970.

[48]*Le Monde*, Nov. 22-23, 1981.

[49]May 21, 1975.

[50]Jan. 24, 1974.

[51]June 19, 1980.

[52]In his book, *Un Peuple de trop sur la terre?* (Paris: Les Presses d'aujourd'hui, 1979), Rabi attacked Israel's policies and the Zionist "establishment."

[53]Sept. 26, 1974.

[54]Legris, "*Le Monde*", p. 147.

[55]May 17, 1974.

[56]Jean Cau, *Lettre ouverte à tout Le Monde* (Paris: A. Michel, 1976), p. 143.

[57]A. Guedj and J. Girault, "*Le Monde,*" *humanisme, objectivité et politique* (Paris: Editions Sociales, 1970), pp. 129-130.

[58]Domenach writes of a "malaise" induced by the "inflexion of a title, the use of punctuation (square brackets, quotation marks), indirect questions, the conditional tense." *Esprit* (April, 1976), p. 771.

[59]See in particular *Le Monde* of March 13, 1980 (p. 4) where the editors in a brief square-bracketed paragraph strongly defend President Giscard d'Estaing. A former member of *Le Monde*'s staff has commented aptly on the newspaper's relation to power: "the power acquired by *Le Monde* leads to its acquisition by power...which immediately implies that there are certain truths that *Le Monde* cannot tell." (Philippe Simonnot, *"Le Monde" et le pouvoir*, Paris: Les Presses d'Aujourd'hui, 1977, p. 222).

[60]*Le Monde*, Sept. 5 1978.

[61]"D'un antisémitisme, l'autre," *L'Arche* (Sept.-Oct.), 1979.

[62]*Le Monde* often used such columns as "Tribune Libre" and "Libres Opinions" as well as the page "Idées" (page 2), to publish the views of "personalities" and alleged experts, many of whom are regular, if not frequent contributors. These columns are supposedly independent of editorial opinion.

[67]"La Pulsion suicidaire," July 2, 1977.

[68]"Portant la Torah, emmaillotée de velours et d'or, comme une idole des temps cananéens."

[69]B.-H. Lévy interviewed in *L'Arche* (February, 1981), p. 41.

[70]Revel, *La Nouvelle censure*, p. 77.

[71]Thibau, *"Le Monde", histoire d'un journal*, p. 18.

[72]In May, 1983, a senior editor of *Le Monde* admitted in a conversation with this

writer that Fauvet, who retired in 1982, was hostile to Jews. He added that the newspaper's attitude toward Israel has undergone a change. A decision was apparently taken to follow President Mitterrand's "more honest" policy line on the Jewish state.

# CHAPTER VI

# The Right: The Old and The New

Since the Dreyfus case, anti-Semitism became for the right in France what anti-clericalism was for the left, a tradition and a unifying banner that could be waved at every opportunity. During the debates over Vichy's treatment of the Jews, which followed the 1978 interview with Darquier de Pellepoix in *L'Express*, the history of right-wing Judeophobia was rediscovered by the French media. The editorialist in a Paris weekly remarked that Darquier "provided the reminder that there was indeed a French tradition of [right-wing] anti-Semitism."[1]

The germs of racism, anti-Semitism and narrow nationalism are deeply rooted in French culture and have spawned a Fascist mentality that predates that of Mussolini and Hitler. Anti-Semitism is "a myth that permeates the entire French ideology. It is the myth in which it is steeped entirely . . . like a ship in its frame."[2] This anti-democratic, chauvinistic and viscerally anti-Semitic ideology rejected democracy as a pernicious "Jewish" concept that granted social and political equality to "foreign races" which did not deserve it, and as a tool to exploit the weakness of the "rooted" French population. If, in the nineteenth century, many of these beliefs were shared by right and left-wing thinkers, by the turn of the century it was primarily the French right that promoted the notion that the malignant nature of the Jew was due to racial factors (although there were racists among Socialists as well).

Historians have stressed France's role in the birth of modern racist theories, "in the formation, elaboration and the spread of the modern concept of race."[3] The contributions of such thinkers as Gobineau and Barrès to the creation of modern racialist philosophy are considerable. Count Arthur de Gobineau (1816-1882), the author of the *Essay on the Inequality of Human Races (1853-5)*, was the father of the belief in the "natural superiority" of "Aryan" races and his work served as a guide to the author of *Mein Kampf*. Gobineau's book has been called "the first, the most embracing, the most accomplished, perhaps, of the breviaries of hatred Europe has produced."[4] Although not specifically anti-Semitic, Gobineau's ideas extolling the virtues of the "Nordic" race were enthusiastically embraced in Germany.

Maurice Barrès (1862-1923), whose writings were to influence several generations of Frenchmen, was another prominent racist. A novelist of note, Barrès also possessed the skill to tie various strands of racial ideology into a unified political vision. He became one of the "most active propagandists of Aryan mythology,"[5] and thought that Captain Dreyfus' guilt was inscribed in "his genes his race, the shape of his skull."[6] Barrès was explicitly anti-Semitic, and wished to purge Christianity of its "vile Judaic ferment." Barrès' anti-Semitism was related to a mystical nationalism, and to the concept of "rootedness" ("enracinement") that the "cosmopolitan" Jew necessarily lacked.

Toward the end of the nineteenth century Edouard Drumont, a publicist whose skilful pen excelled in vituperation, performed an intellectual balancing act that succeeded in uniting the racist, anti-Semitic concepts of both the left and the right in one book. In his *La France juive* (1886), which outsold almost every other publication in the century, and was read avidly by cabdrivers and aristocrats alike, Drumont alleged the existence of a Jewish bid to take over Europe, and portrayed the Jews as the source of every social, political and economic problem that beset France. Serialized by the largest circulation daily, *Le Petit Journal* — which also gave away copies of Drumont's book as contest prizes — *La France juive* also claimed that Jews were spies, traitors and carriers of disease. The book, soon translated in Germany and Poland, charged that Jews corrupt and exploit the naive and tolerant French.

As a crusader with God on his side Drumont considered it a religious duty to drive the Jews out of France. His use of the clergy and the Catholic press, his praise for the Church's past persecutions against Jews, gave his campaign overtones of another Inquisition. It was a measure of Drumont's success that such popular Catholic dailies as *La Croix* accepted anti-Semitism as a doctrine, and that many priests "seemed to have regarded hatred of the Jews as part of the Catholic faith."[7] A mixture of falsehood and piety, distorted statistics about Jewish wealth and wild exaggerations about its influence on the French economy, was combined in

*La France juive* with the traditional Christ-killer charge.

In his appeal for action Drumont managed to unite "all the anti-Judaic and anti-Semitic notions expressed before him and to elevate the Jewish myth to an ideology and a political method."[8] Under the banner of anti-Semitism Drumont spurred on a movement that combined anti-capitalism and capitalists, Catholics and atheists, workers and their bosses, in a prefiguration of National Socialism.[9] Thirty years before Hitler's *Mein Kampf*, *La France juive* called for the removal of Jews from Aryan societies. Not surprisingly, Drumont's book was utilized by the right-wing, anti-Semitic movements between the two World Wars and during the Vichy period.

It was Drumont's campaign, with the unprecedented publicity given to it by the press, that prepared the way for the Dreyfus Affair and the transformation of anti-Semitism in France from an element of Socialist ideology to a political vehicle of the right. The royalists saw in *La France juive* — with its relentless attacks on the Republic and harping on the financial scandals allegedly made possible by the parliamentary system — perfect tool to bolster their efforts to reinstate the monarchy. For the emerging ultra-nationalist forces that were soon to coalesce under the ideology of "Action Française," the castigation of a despised foreign element, sapping the nation's strength, was a welcome slogan confirming important tenets of their ideology.

During the tensely-fought anti-republican campaign, the monarchists, the Church and the army used anti-Semitism as the battleground on which the political future of France was fought out. The usefulness of the Jew in the power struggle was explained by Charles Maurras, who was soon to become one of the intellectual guides of his generation: "without this providential anti-Semitism everything seems impossible or frightfully difficult. With it, everything settles, becomes smooth and simple. If one were not an anti-Semite through patriotic sentiment, one would have to become one merely to take advantage of it."[10] A study of the psychological causes of anti-Semitism argues that when there is a deep need for social fusion, a desire to forge new emotional ties among individuals, a common hatred, such as the hatred of the Jew, becomes a powerful means to fill it.[11]

Charles Maurras, an admirer of Drumont, was among the influential instigators of anti-Semitism who came to the fore at the end of the 1890s. Few men had a more profound impact on French ideology in the twentieth century. A poet, essayist and journalist, Maurras (1886-1952), made the Jew a symbol of everything he despised in the society of his day. Elaborating on Drumont's clichés, he viewed the Jew as a "foreign element" in the national body and a threat to the unity of the country. For Maurras the monarchist, who advocated order, discipline and unity, the Jew represented a democracy that allowed unscrupulous financiers to conduct their affairs unmolested. "Jewish power, "he wrote," its ability to acquire and keep wealth comes from the fact that it is a state within a state."[12] The Jew is a pernicious creature that "gnaws, sucks dry and tyrannizes the country."[13] Short of advocating their extermination, Maurras wished to keep Jews in a lowly position, refusing them even French citizenship: "it is not a question of saying 'Death to the Jews'...but 'down with the Jews' because they have risen too high in our country."[14]

Through the monarchist, extreme-right organization "Action Française," which he helped found in 1899, Maurras exercised a major influence on French life for close to half a century. As an editor of the daily, L'Action Française — which acquired a reputation for its elegant style and brilliant contributors — he produced, along with monarchist propaganda, a steady stream of anti-Semitic diatribes. Maurras' anti-Jewish activities did not cease until August, 1944, when the newspaper was closed down at the end of the Vichy period. He was condemned to life imprisonment for his collaboration with the Germans.

Following the Russian revolution, a new element was added to the collection of anti-Semitic clichés, the "Judeo-Bolshevik plot" to spread Marxism in the world. The Jew was not only a foreigner and a parasite, he was also a radical and a subverter of the established order of society. This, and other topics, were comprised in the steady dose of anti-Jewish hatred that was dispensed by L'Action Française and a growing number of other ultranationalist publications. By the late 1920s, Maurras' movement had gained the participation of some notable intellectuals as well as backing in large segments of the printed media.

The influx of East European Jews in search of employment provided new grist for the anti-Semitic mill. In a difficult economic situation Fascist leagues sprouted. The 1930s saw the birth of an authentic French Fascist party, "Le Parti Populaire Français," led by a former Communist, Jacques Doriot. His newspaper, La Liberté, received financial support from Nazi Germany. Significantly, Doriot's party was supported by such brilliant intellectuals as Pierre Drieu de la Rochelle, who served as a member of its political bureau. On the streets there were occasional attacks against Jews, and in the parliament Xavier Vallat, who was to become Vichy's first Commissioner for Jewish Affairs, indulged in anti-Semitic outbursts against the Jewish Socialist leader, Léon Blum.

When, in 1936, Blum became the first Jewish Prime Minister of France, the anti-Semites were enraged. Maurras entitled one of his anti-Semitic editorials, "France Under the Jew." Before Blum's government was forced to resign, the National Assembly was the scene of open anti-Semitic agitation during which right-wing parliamentarians shouted, "Death to the Jews." In the 1930s, anti-Semitic writings "covered the market from the high-quality product to the cheap, mass-produced article."[15] Newspapers like Le Soleil published "economic" reports showing Jewish "control" of property, the press and advertising. Respected writers openly voiced anti-Semitic notions. In the four or five years that preceded the war, "80% of the Paris population that could form an idea was anti-Semitic, from the Communists of Billancourt to the royalists of 'Action Française'."[16] Although no doubt exaggerated, this estimate may not have been too far off the mark.

After the war, the revelation of the horrors of Hitler's extermination camps, and the near-excommunication of the right for its collaboration with the Nazi occupiers, appeared to have brought anti-Semitism to its lowest level in this century. Yet, already in 1946, a dispute over the restoration of Jewish property became the occasion of anti-Semitic agitation. The Jews who escaped from Hitler's crematoria returned to find out that the property that they left behind belonged legally to their non-Jewish neighbours. Those who had either taken over Jewish property during the war, or had bought it at the lowest price from Jews fleeing for their lives, refused to return it to its previous owners. A group calling itself "The Association of Buyers in Good Faith," conducted a public campaign to justify their retention of the war-time acquisitions, and in the process resorted to anti-Semitic arguments.

Since the 1950s, there has been a slow, sometimes imperceptible, yet persistent drive to exonerate Nazism. Some sought the rehabilitation of Marshal Pétain and demanded a transfer of his ashes to the National Cemetery. Veterans of the French SS Division, "Charlemagne," sought to revise the image of National Socialism. Some of them published books about their war exploits which portrayed World War II as a conflict between chivalric armies, and omitted any mention of the Nazi atrocities. The debate over a French withdrawal from Indochina was also accompanied by anti-Semitic overtones. During the negotiations he conducted in Geneva in 1954, Pierre Mendès-France was accused by the right of "selling out," of betraying France, and his Jewish origins were openly referred to in the National Assembly as proof of this "betrayal." In 1955, when Mendès-France was forced to resign as Prime Minister, his "Jewishness" was widely believed to have been a factor in the resignation.

The resistance to French disengagement from the colonial war in Algeria was led by right-wing elements that saw in the fight for "French Algeria" a chance to return to the political mainstream. Such organisations as the OAS ("Organisation de l'Armée Secrète") and the "Delta Commando" which attempted to assassinate De Gaulle, although not overtly anti-Semitic, harbored a number of Fascists. After the withdrawal from Algeria the importance of these groups declined, although some organizational ties were maintained. Even De Gaulle's para-military group, S.A.C. ("Service d'Action Civique"), formed to combat leftism, counted many former right-wing extremists in its ranks.

The 1960s also gave birth to several extreme right-wing organisations with such names as the "Charles Martel Club," "Honor of the Police," "The Peiper Group" (named after an assassinated Nazi) and "Order and New Justice." These neo-Nazi groups held meetings in remote country estates with the participation of German Nazis and trained in close-combat tactics and marksmanship wearing full Nazi uniforms. In recent years, the most prominent French neo-Nazi group involved in anti-Jewish terror, FANE (acronym for "Federaton for National European Action") openly revealed its ties to the international Nazi movement. Like its main rival, "L'Oeuvre Française," FANE considered Israel as an enemy equal to Communism and fed on left-wing anti-Zionism and the fashionable anti-Americanism. Marc Fredricksen, the leader of FANE, declared that "Europe is threatened by American and Israeli imperialism."[17]

In addition to its anti-Zionism, FANE used its publication, *Notre Europe* (one of its contributors was the editor of the Vichy anti-Semitic sheet *Pilori*), to warn Frenchmen of the Jewish peril,[18] and to proclaim that the Holocaust never existed. During one of his appearances in court, Fredriksen claimed that "the Final Solution was invented by the Jews to obtain substantial war reparations from the Germans."[19] His organizaton charged that French culture was in Jewish hands. FANE's activities also included the distribution of pamphlets with such titles as, "The Auschwitz Lie," "Christ Was Not a Jew," and "The Talmud Unmasked." This neo-Nazi group has worked with "Oeuvre Française" to form an "Edouard Drumont Club," and proclaimed the nineteenth-century anti-Semite as one of its "old members." During Fredricksen's trial a witness remarked: "FANE would not have developed if the ground had not been prepared for years."[20]

In the 1950s and 1960s, the publication of novels dealing with Jewish history stirred some unrepentent Vichy supporters back to life. André Schwarz-Bart's *The Last of the Just* (1959) and Jean-François Steiner's *Treblinka* (1966) provoked passionate debates that prefigured the controversies in the late 1970s. Already in 1961, a well-known novelist and critic, Maurice Bardèche, wrote that in concentration camps that have been transformed into museums "torture scenes have been built in places where they never existed," and that this proved that history "can be fabricated."[21] A populist movement founded by Pierre Poujade in 1956 was spreading anti-Semitic propaganda that was "a veritable aggression against French Jews in the purest Goebbels style."[22] One of Poujade's supporters who gained a seat in the National Assembly, Jean-Marie Le Pen, later became the leader of the the extreme-right National Front.

In the 1970s, when the anti-Zionism of the left had made itself felt in the public forum, the extreme-right, sensing a new atmosphere of permissiveness, crawled back into the open. At a meeting held in Paris, in May 1970, with 3000 right-wingers in attendance, speakers called for the restoration of the honor of Pétain and of the collaborationist, anti-Semitic writers, Céline and Brasillach. A few years later, the right gained access to the high-circulation press when Robert Hersant, a man who had collaborated with Germans and was known as a militant anti-Semite, acquired such major newspapers as *Le Figaro*, *L'Aurore* and *France-Soir* (the highest-circulation evening daily in France). While building a press empire Hersant also managed to get elected to the National Assembly.

Interviewed in a Jewish publication in 1979, the editor of the right-wing weekly *Minute* criticized Jews for "playing pernicious roles in the countries in which they live."[23] He also accused French Jewry of double loyalty and of disrespect for French nationalist sentiment. The editor of the more moderately rignt-wing *Aspects de la France*, Pierre Pujo, reproached French Jews for "their double allegiance and their tendency to form a state within a state."[24]

In spite of a 1972 law forbidding incitement of racial discrimination, the so-called "Pleven law," the various right-wing weeklies, whose combined circulation approached 250,000, found ways to besmirch the Jews without naming them. In 1975, a right-wing organization, angered by a proposal to legalize abortions, launched a campaign against the Minister of Health, Simone Veil, branding her as the "Jewish abortionist" and covering her with "particularly ignoble insults."[25]

With a verve that displayed a new feeling of legitimacy, segments of the right joined the chorus of anti-Zionist propaganda (although some rightists expressed ambiguous support for Israel). The young right-wingers of the 1970s called themselves anti-Zionists, and denounced, as did their opponents on the left, Israeli "colonialists and exploiters." Pierre Sidos, the leader of the extreme right-wing "Oeuvre Française," received financial support from the Arabs "for having discovered that Zionism and Communism are two sides of the same threat."[26] The same leader wrote in 1974 of an "obligation to put a definitive end to the Rothschilds."[27] A reborn "Action Française" called for the "destruction of the State of Israel and a totally pro-Arab French policy," while plastering Paris walls with posters proclaiming: "Palestine Will be Victorious!"[28]

Pierre Sidos summarized today's version of *The Protocols of the Elders of Zion* as a "plan" for Jewish domination of the world. The French Fascist incorporated into the old myth the role of the modern State of Israel and its alledged "expansionist" designs, that seemed plausible to the new generation exposed to right and left-wing anti-Semitism. Sidos defined Zionism as an ideology that is "at once false, aggressive and domineering ... intent on progressive expansion ... from the Nile to the Euphrates to the end of the planet, with a capital common to the Hebrew State and the entire Zionized world: the Judaicized city of Jerusalem."[29] Another right-wing leader, François Duprat, revealed that he had contacts with the Arab League and that his movement had been promoting the "Liberation of Palestine."[30] Duprat also issued pamphlets denying the Holocaust, maintained contacts with German Nazis and published books bearing such titles as *The Waffen-SS, The Race* and *Hitler's Europe.*[31].

Although the mainstream of the French Catholic Church has worked for reconciliation with the Jews, elements in the Church remained loyal to its nineteenth-century staunchly conservative and anti-Semitic tradition. Some French Catholics continued to see the Jews as a disruptive element threatening French traditions. On the spiritual level, Judaism was still viewed as a heresy that was difficult to come to terms with. In the 1970s, the extreme-right Catholic group known as the "Office," a French version of "Opus Dei," was involved in the distribution of a new printing of the *Protocols of the Elders of Zion*. The fanatical "Christ-King" movement distributed monthly 40,000 copies of its bulletin in which Frenchmen could read accusations, by a certain Abbé Georges of Nantes, that Jews were deicides, after all. In a highly publicized trial held in the city of Troyes, this priest, echoing medieval Christian exhortations, insisted that "the only event that can change the hereditary malediction into benediction is the conversion of the Jews to the Christ-King."[32] The president of the League of Human Rights expressed shock over the fanaticism of the "Christ-King" movement.[33]

In 1981, the appointment of a converted Jew, Mgr. Lustiger, to head the diocese of the French capital was seen by the moderate, right-wing publication, *Rivarol*, as part of a Jewish plot to demolish the Catholic Church. After the October, 1980, synagogue bombing a right-wing spokesman counselled Jews to keep a "low profile." Commenting on the mass protest demonstration that followed the explosion, a spokesman for a right-wing group declared: "On October 7, 1980, hundreds of thousands of people have contributed to the rebirth of anti-Semitism in France for decades [to come]."[34]

In addition to the openly Fascist elements, a survey of right-wing strength in France must include the more discrete, but potentially no less dangerous, large segment of the population that still identifies with a form of Maurrassian ideology. This group is made up of highly educated individuals who rarely show open bigotry, but whose "sly, discrete Fascism and a certain noble manner embellished by a concern for the humble and the poor are more significant."[35] In the late 1970s, the old right also drew inspiration from a new school of thought that promoted a sophisticated form of racism, the "Nouvelle Droite."

In June, 1979, the French mass circulation press uncovered a new right-wing movement that had been in existence for ten years in semi-clandestinity and whose members had managed to infiltrate the upper echelons of government bureaucracy and the cabinets of some ministries. Calling itself "La Nouvelle Droite"

("New Right"), the group, composed of graduates of France's elite educational institutions, espoused a sophisticated ideology that captured the imagination of the pundits in the media, who created a wave of publicity around it. Only thirty years after Hitler, a French weekly noted, such concepts as eugenics, malthusianism, inequality of races, xenophobia and the need for a supreme leader have reappeared.[36] The advocacy of such old right-wing notions as anti-cosmopolitanism, rootedness in regional culture, and the cult of the "exceptional" man, reappeared as virtues.

Cleverly disguising old reactionary tenets, the leaders of the "New Right" disclaimed adherence to racist or anti-Semitic ideology. They preferred to speak merely of "social differences," and denied backing segregation of groups or individuals on the basis of ethnic and class factors. Playing on ideas that appealed to the new generation infatuated with the self, "authenticity," and the belief in the infinite capacities of modern science, the NR projected the image of a serious school of thought with faith in the future. Its quest for roots and focus on the biological sciences as the panacea for all social problems, contrasted with the pessimistic forecasts issuing from other intellectual circles.

In essence, the NR claimed that in order to save itself from progressive deterioration and eventual collapse, western European societies must promote a rediscovery of their Indo-European and Celtic roots. They must reject Judeo-Christianity with its belief in the equality of all humans and heed the findings of sociobiology and genetics in order to improve their natural stock. France, and its sister "Indo-European" nations, must also rediscover the old values of courage, discipline and sacrifice, and reject the mercantile mentality that flows to them from such trade-oriented, utilitarian societies as the United States. In order to achieve its goals, Europe must also oppose egalitarianism and support the development of ruling elites capable of governing efficiently. Because man was not born equal he must allow the best of his species to exercise their talents.

The formation of these elites is heavily dependent on a return to the pre-Christian European ideals. Europe must rediscover its own roots, the tradition of the pagan gods that symbolizes, the Indo-European Occident in its purest form. It is this ancestry that embodies the ethic of sacrifice, strength and self-confidence that is necessary for the rejuvenation of a declining Europe. Paganism, with its multiplicity of gods, guaranteed tolerance and formed a barrier against totalitarianism, tyranny, and crippling feelings of guilt that were imposed on Western man by monotheistic Judeo-Christianity. Paganism also legitimized varieties of worship, thus allowing for greater self-development, for more daring, and for the kind of heroism depicted in Celtic and Nordic myths. This freedom, combined with a closeness to natural instincts, encouraged the emergence of differences, the survival and nurturing of the best and the fittest, and thus a higher possibility of identifying elites. Polytheism, exalting form and beauty, gave birth to art and freedom of thought.[37] Unfortunately, according to the concepts of the NR, this idyllic state was brutally interrupted by the imposition of Judeo-Christianity, which alienated Europe from itself.

Judeo-Christian monotheism, branded by the New Right as a "sectarian myth," a "disease of the mind," has sapped the vital energies of pagan Europe. The indictment against Biblical monotheism, with its "angry God," carried with it the more serious charge of totalitarianism. NR ideologues stated unequivocally: "totalitarianism made its appearance in history only with the advent of Judeo-Christianity."[38] The leader of a major NR group refined this claim by placing the blame at the feet of Abraham: "totalitarianism was born the day the monotheist idea appeared, implying the submission of the human being to a single God... everything began historically with Abraham ... the appeal to fanaticism and intolerance has been ringing since the time of Abraham."[39]

The monotheistic faith, the NR claims, also brought with it egalitarianism, which encourages mediocrity and lack of effort. It is the angry Jewish God who encouraged intolerance and restricted man's mental and physical freedom. Egalitarianism is an obstacle to progress and to the health of society, it is a foreign, "Jewish" element that spoiled a natural, vibrant organism. Although the ideologues of the NR are careful never to single out Jews as their enemies — they always speak of Judeo-Christianity — there is little doubt who is designated as the real culprit. Alain de Benoist, the uncontested leader of the NR, asked, "who are these strangers who have transformed our house, causing us to lose in the darkness of passing time the very consciousness of who we are?"[40] The answer de Benoist failed to give could only be: Jews and "their" Christ.

Alain de Benoist has also written that Celtic, warring, aggressive Europe is suffering today from a lack of selectivity and a lack of elite leadership, due to two-thousand year-old Judeo-Christian "occupation" that brought from the East "incapacitating and guilt-engendering" myths, excessive respect for life and social justice. NR periodicals contain references to the "ideological poison" that destroyed the world of antiquity, and "implanted itself in the heart" of European civilization.[41]

Repeatedly, "Judeo-Christian" monotheism is blamed by the NR for the mental and social "paralysis" of Europe. One of the sympathizers of the NR ideology, an award-winning writer of considerable talent, has spelled out the source of the "evil" more explicitly. Jean-Edern Hallier, who like a number of other French intellectuals has recently rediscovered the virtues of ethnic, regional roots, has written that he cannot be a Celt without being "anti-Judaic," although he is careful to point out, he is not anti-Semitic.[42] Because Judaism carries the germ of Christian mysticism, Hallier added, "more than ever, we must *exterminate* metaphysical Judaism."[43] Apparently, for Hallier the adjective "metaphysical" provided a sufficient alibi against charges that his statement could incite anti-Jewish violence. Hallier has also branded the Jewish custom of circumcision as a symbol of Judaism's stress on sexuality and hygiene to the detriment of spirituality, and claimed that the Jewish God is above all a persecutor.

Men were created unequal, the NR proclaims, and it is Judaism's and Christianity's insistence on human equality that is responsible for such evils as race-mixing, genetic disorders and pernicious ideologies as Marxism, which is merely a lay version of oppressive Jewish religious thought, of Biblical messianism. Judeo-Christian egalitarianism also encourages mediocrity, submission and depersonalization. Louis Pauwels, another well-known proponent of NR thinking, argued that "the historic and cultural destiny of a society depends more on elites than on the masses . . . a society is based on 'meritocracies' and not on an egalitarianism of natures and destinies."[44]

According to NR philosophers the findings of modern biology show that inequalities among men are hereditary, that intelligence is primarily determined by genetic factors, that the theory which postulates that an improved environment leads to equal opportunity and an eradication of differences is based on flawed information. NR critics perceived both the danger and the intent of such notions: "one does not preach a crusade against equality by brandishing the weapons of history and the shield of biology without waking the demons of violence, domination, scorn and racism."[45] A 1971 issue of *Nouvelle école*, the principal publication of the NR, contained an article which advocated abortion and euthanesia, the elimination of pathological cases for the sake of "programming" the ideal human specimen.

The origins of the new movement give credence to the contention that the NR is to some extent a reincarnation of the "Old Right" which, conscious of the fact that crudely racist, elitist ideas are less likely to have wide appeal, has decided to modernize its tenets. Alain de Benoist has admitted past membership in such extreme right-wing groups as "Europe Action" and "Jeune Nation." Some NR leaders have been associated with other extremist and monarchist organizations. The main NR group, G.R.E.C.E. (the clever French acronym for "Group for Research and Study of European Civilization" which alludes to ancient, "European" Greece), lists among its sponsors a former Vichy collaborator and members of the editorial staff of such racist and neo-Fascist periodicals as *Mankind Quarterly* and *Neue Anthropologie*. G.R.E.C.E. has also sponsored a lecture by the fascist writer, Maurice Bardèche, who has provided perhaps the most explicit proof of the affinity between the old and the new right. "This *realpolitik* of the right that the generation of Alain de Benoist proposes, "he wrote," is perhaps the only path left open to us to leave the 'ghetto' the right finds itself in."[46] The NR, wrote a prominent political scientist, shields the ideas of the old right.[47]

The NR, which denies that it constitutes a political group, is clearly bent on a long-range strategy. It has acknowledged borrowing the concepts of the Italian Marxist philosopher, Antonio Gramsci, for whom political revolution must be preceded by an intensive cultural campaign aiming to sensitize and to indoctrinate. Such a campaign eventually renders even extreme political ideas acceptable. G.R.E.C.E. portrays istelf as just another cultural association interested in new trends in the art and sciences. Realizing that modern Western societies are more vulnerable to veiled political discourse than to direct political propaganda, the NR, unlike the old right, eschews direct, illicit political action. In the long run, this makes the new movement all the more dangerous.

The NR's ultimate ambitions for power are confirmed by its creation of a group with the objective of gaining influence among the military. "Nation Armée," a bulletin of the group, innocently states its aims as geared "to assume better liaison and comprehension between the nation and those in charge of its defense."[48] The journal, *Nouvelle ecole*, was more explicit in its advice to members of G.R.E.C.E. concerning its aims: "We urge our members to mix...

to get involved in any activity provided that the possiblities are promising...editorial offices of newspapers, magazines, the direction of scientific organizations ... What we need are influential men who hold positions in decision-making circles today and even more tomorrow."[49]

The former editor of the weekly, *Les Nouvelles littéraires*, J.-F. Kahn, has remarked that the NR has proven to be remarkably skillful in covering its tracks. In spite of its outspoken opposition to totalitarianism, it is in fact against liberal democracies fostering educational systems that suppress potential elites. Kahn points out that the NR cannot be in favor of universal suffrage and at the same time for a semi-dictatorial leader, a "guide" to the nation. These contradictions do not remove the fact that there exists in France an intellectually sophisticated right-wing movement that repeats in a veiled form slogans from a recent ugly past: racism, anti-liberalism and hostility to Judaism. Although the difference between the old and the new right-wingers is more than tactical in nature, the notions they both share cannot be reassuring.

The NR's insistence on "Judeo-Christianity's" role in Europe's misfortunes, in fact on the Jews' guilt in the spoliation of Europe, tends to picture the Jew as the pernicious intruder, the "other". At the same time, the valorisation of Aryan races depreciates the "invading" Semitic race, branding it as inferior. This negative image of the "Semite" is expressed in such phrases as, "we have decided to identify with the European past, not with the *oriental mirage*."[50] The term "oriental mirage," vague enough perhaps to serve as an alibi for outright racial defamation, it is not sufficiently opaque, however, to disguise a derogatory connotation. More explicit is the definition of the Jewish ethic as a "neurotic edifice."[51]

No one in the NR had denied harboring anti-Semitic sentiments more vigorously than Alain de Benoist. Yet, in 1978, he attended a conference of the anti-Semitic "World Anti-Communist League" and expressed his enthusiasm for Arthur de Gobineau's racist theories. Moreover, de Benoist listed the militant anti-Semite, Pierre Drieu de la Rochelle, as one of the NR's ancestors, and has expressed admiration for his journal, *Les Derniers jours*, which is studded with anti-Semitic comments.

The idea that the Russian revolution was the result of a "Judeo-Bolshevik" plot is a standard anti-Semitic canard. The NR has repeated this myth in a somewhat more sophisticated manner: "Orthodox Marxist theory reproduced in laicized form the theory of *Christian* history, whereas neo-Marxist or Freudo-Marxist theory more closely reproduces classical Jewish thought."[52] Other tell-tale signs of its hostility to Jews emanate from the praise heaped in *Nouvelle école* on the official sculptor of the Third Reich, Arno Breker, and references to the authority of George Montadon, a racist anthropologist used by Vichy to implement its "Aryanization" program, as an authoritative source.[53]

By stating in *Le Figaro-magazine* that Nazism was just another totalitarianism among many in history, its editor, Louis Pauwels, indicated a refusal to accept Hitler's methodical extermination of the Jews as unique.[54] He also showed his insensitivity to the Jewish tragedy by publishing, side by side, photos of corpses in the Buchenwald concentration camp and of German victims of the Allied bombing of Dresden.[55] Moreover, although the NR has repeatedly focused on the Russian Gulags, it is difficult to find in its writings an explicit denunciation of Nazi concentration camps. *Eléments*, the organ of the NR "Club de l'Horloge" ("Clock Club"), has devoted an issue to Germany in which the aggressor in two world wars is depicted as a victim that had lost twelve million men, that was "bled white" twice in this century. In the same periodical, the NR issued an appeal to the "great Germany," calling upon it to "awake," unite and return to its past "greatness" to lead European reconstruction.[56]

Some of the NR's critics have noted that the "idea of a cohesive Indo-European culture founded on the cult of energy and heroism resembles a great deal what Hitler was saying in *Mein Kampf*."[57] Others have accused it of promoting anti-Semitism that is hiding behind a smokescreen in which the term Judeo-Christianity is merely a euphemism for "Jew" and "Judaism." Although overt anti-Semitism is difficult to detect in NR literature "the NR is totally and knowingly guilty, because its condemnation of Judeo-Christianity is a rhetorical disguise of its anti-Semitism and its congenital anti-Judaism."[58] Following the bombing of the rue Copernic synagogue, *Le Monde* wrote that "the resurrection of neo-Nazism is undoubtedly linked to the right's ideological rebirth spurred on by the leaders of the New Right."[59]

The penetration of the NR into the mass media, its ability to project a learned, sensible image, has resulted in the legitimation of quasi-Fascist concepts in the eyes of an unsuspecting public. The real danger of the NR is its methodical effort to build an ideological infrastructure, modelled on Gramsci's blueprints, which will eventually render Fascist ideas legitimate. Cloaked in respectability, the NR seems to be able to demonstrate that Fascists do not necessarily wear jackboots and brown shirts. The danger of the NR lies also in the fact that it has "installed a rhetorical and ideological apparatus by means of which the French bourgeoisie can give itself a conscience."[60] In a land that places great value on intellect, where intellectual discussion has often served as a justification for the diffusion of abhorrent beliefs, movements like the New Right are an obvious potential threat to those whose ancestry lacks "pure" European origins.

In the early 1980s, an extreme-right movement, calling itself "Le Front National," emerged as a political force to be reckoned with. The party's leader, Jean-Marie Le Pen, a charismatic demagogue, denied any association with extremists and presented himself as a conservative politician, in the Reagan mould. He was for law and order and against Communism, government intervention in social and political life, "decadence" in French culture, and "deviants" (such as homosexuals). Le Pen denied that his call for the expulsion of migrant workers was racist, although he said that "there are too many foreigners in France and far too many Arabs." In a climate of insecurity and high unemployment, often blamed on foreigners, the slogan, "La France aux Français" and Le Pen's image of resoluteness contrasted with the government's hesitant response to the situation.

Although Le Pen has claimed that he is against anti-Jewish discrimination and has not displayed recently any overt anti-Semitism, Jews were worried about the future direction of his movement. Some noted that the favorite targets at National Front meetings were invariably Robert Badinter, the Minister of Justice, Simone Veil, former Minister of Health, and the Archbishop of Paris, Mgr. Lustiger, all of whom are of Jewish origin. The attacks against Veil have been particularly distasteful. The author of an abortion bill, she has been accused by Le Pen of aiming to carry out a "genocide" against unborn French babies. In the context of the well-known fact that Veil is a survivor of a Nazi concentration camp, the term, "genocide" was invidious.

Romain Marie, Le Pen's closest lieutenant, who was one of the 10 members of the National Front elected to the European Parliament, referred to the leadership of the Russian revolution as an "international of assassins that was composed essentially of Jews," and complained that there are "powers in France" for which "the interests of Judaism are more important than those of French society."[61]

Elected to the National Assembly in 1956 on the ticket of the populist Poujade movement, Le Pen created his own party in 1968. Although he proclaims himself a friend of Israel, many of his supporters in the past were vehemently anti-Semitic, sympathized with neo-Nazi organizations, and belonged to such groups as "New Europe" and "New Order." Le Pen claims that he has dropped these allies, but the daily newspaper, *Présent*, the organ of the NF, resorted to anti-Semitic imagery. Its editor, François Brigneau, denounced Badinter's alleged laxity toward criminals and charged that he supported "the nomad against the settler, the cosmopolitan against the indigenous...the murderer against the murdered, the outcast against a society which has for so long done without Badinter and his tribe." He added: "the only thing French about such men is where they live. When we stop and consider to what extent they have taken control of this country, it is indeed time for us to be afraid."[62] Romain Marie echoed *The Protocols of the Elders of Zion* when he wrote about "the tendency of Jews to monopolize all the highest positions in the Western nations . . . the modern world is experiencing a new intrusion of the Jewish phenomenon."[63] Arnaud de Lassus, a prominent supporter of Le Pen, told a Paris gathering of 2,000 that Jews were one of the four "superpowers colonizing France," and that Judaism "permeates" French politics.[64]

Le Pen himself has expressed puzzlement over the need to protect synagogues more than non-Jewish premises, disregarding anti-Jewish terrorist attacks and vandalism. He has also refused to condemn the open racism of his closest supporters, and has remarked that he has "no taste" for the art of Chagall or for such politicians as Mendès-France, Badinter, and Veil. Two decades earlier, in 1958, his distaste for Mendès-France was more blunt when he said that the Jewish politician provoked an "almost physical revulsion."

A French tribunal noted in connection with a suit filed by Le Pen against a daily, that slogans such as "Badinter, Juif" (this term still carries strong pejorative connotations), and "Veil to the Oven," are often chanted at Le Pen's political rallies. The court in Amiens, which rejected Le Pen's complaint at being called "a disciple of Franco and Hitler," declared that the NF, "tolerates passively the multiplication of public manifestations linked to anti-Semitism and Nazi ideology during its political meetings without taking measures to prevent or stigmatize them."[65]

The potential threat of the NF lies also in some of the alliances it has forged and some of the professional political activists it has attracted. Le Pen has drawn support from such business groups as the National Centre of Independents and Farmers (CNIP) and from the Movement of Small Industries. He has established committees in all the rural regions of France as well as in large cities. The organizational basis of the National Front has benefited from the presence of several highly experienced professional organizers. Jean-Marie Le Chevalier acquired his expertise in party work as director of the Cabinet of Jacques Dominati, the General Secretary of former President Giscard d'Estaing's party. Jean-Pierre Stirbois is an expert in political mass organization. In Toulouse and Marseilles seasoned leaders of the RPR and UDF, the two main parties in the Giscard d'Estaing administration, joined the Le Pen bandwagon.

The reaction of the Jewish community to the Le Pen movement has been subdued. Privately many are worried. Some Jews, particularly those with leftist leanings, have called for Jewish participation in the new "fight against Fascism." Although the Chief Rabbi of Dijon called Le Pen "a Nazi and a devil," the President of CRIF, the main political arm of French Jewry, Théo Klein, was less direct: "we know the meaning of some of Le Pen's statements concerning us ... Let us turn our backs on him and recall that our history teaches tolerance ... and respect for the strangers among us."[66] He also said, however, that Le Pen "reminds us of certain aspects of the period that preceded Vichy."[67]

## Notes

[1]*Le Nouvel observateur*, Nov. 6-12, 1978.

[2]B.-H. Lévy, *L'Idéologie française*, p. 108.

[3]*Ibid.*, p. 98. Lévy borrowed this and other findings from the seminal work of Zeev Sternhell.

[4]*Ibid.*, p. 106.

[5]*Ibid.*, p. 110.

[6]*Ibid.*

[7]Malcolm Hay, *Europe and the Jews* (Boston: Beacon Press, 1961), p. 185. To prove that the Jews are an immoral and inferior race Drumont relied heavily on the writings of the noted historian and philologist, Ernest Renan. See J. Katz, *From Prejudice to Destruction, Anti-Semitism, 1700-1933* (Cambridge: Harvard University Press, 1980), p. 295.

[8]M. Winock, "Edouard Drumont et l'antisémitisme en France avant l'Affaire

Dreyfus," *Esprit*, no. 403 (May, 1971), p. 1097.

[9]*Ibid.*, p. 1100.

[10]cited in Sternhell, *La Droite révolutionnaire*, p. 214.

[11]S. Friedländer, *L'Antisémitisme nazi* (Paris: Seuil, 1971), p. 48.

[12]*Dictionnaire politique et critique*, Vol. II (Paris: La Cité des Libres, 1932), p. 359.

[13]*Ibid.*, p. 353.

[14]*Ibid.*, p. 351.

[15]J.S. McClelland, *The Jewish Chronicle*, June 19, 1970.

[16]L. Rebatet, "D'un Céline l'autre," *L.F. Céline, Cahiers de l'herne*, no. 6 (1972), p. 43.

[17]*Le Monde*, Feb. 6, 1981.

[18]*Les Nouvelles littéraires*, July 3, 1980.

[19]*Ibid.*, Sept. 22, 1980.

[20]*Le Monde*, Nov. 6, 1980.

[21]*Nuremberg ou la terre promise*, p. 146, cited in J. Plumyène and R. Lasierra, *Les Fascismes français, 1923-1963* (Paris: Seuil, 1963), p. 209.

[22]Plumyène and Laisierra, *Les Fascismes français*, p. 241.

[23]François Brigneau interviewed in *L'Arche* (Sept.-Oct. 1979).

[24]*Ibid.*

[25]Gregory Pons, *Les Rats noirs* (Paris: J.-C. Simoën, 1977), p. 138.

[26]*Ibid.*, p. 37.

[27]*Ibid.*, p. 39.

[28]*Ibid.*, p. 199.

[29]*Ibid.*, p. 38.

[30]*Ibid.*, p. 65.

[31]*Ibid.*, p. 72.

[32]*La Contre-réforme catholique*, Jan. 1975, cited in Pons, *Les Rats noirs*, p. 165.

[33]*La Terre retrouvée*, Feb. 15, 1975.

[34]*Le Monde*, Oct. 9, 1980.

[35]B.-H. Lévy, *L'Arche* (February, 1981), p. 37.

[36]*Le Nouvel observateur*, July 2-8, 1979.

[37]A. de Benoist, *Les Idées de l'endroit* (Paris: Editions Libres Hallier, 1979), p. 187.

[38]A. de Benoist quoted in M. Calef, "La Valse des plaintes," *Le Monde*, Oct. 15, 1980.

[39]Pierre Vial, quoted in *Le Monde*, Dec. 11, 1979.

[40]Cited in J. Brunn, *La Nouvelle Droite* (Paris: Nouvelles Editions Oswald, 1979), p. 14.

[41]*Eléments* (Aug. 1973), p. 3.

[42]"La Celtitude," *Art press international*, no. 26 (1979), p. 6. In the same issue of *Art press*, Julia Kristeva denounced the "neo-pagan anti-Judeo-Christian" crusade, "that hardly differs from that of the Nazis." The noted literary scholar also considered the new matriarchal cult — opposed to the patriarchally-oriented Judaism — as a "more or less conscious anti-Semitism." (pp. 6-7).

[43]*Art press international*, p. 6. Emphasis added.

[44]Cited in Brunn, *La Nouvelle Droite*, p. 308.

[45]F.-H. de Virieu, in Brunn, *La Nouvelle Droite*, p. 184.

[46]*Défense de l'occident*, no. 170 (December, 1979), p. 29, quoted in P.-A. Taguieff, "L'Heritage nazi," *Les Nouveaux cahiers*, no. 69 (Spring, 1981), p. 5.

[47]Annie Kriegel, *Le Figaro*, July 10, 1979.

[48]Cited in Brunn, *La Nouvelle Droite*, p. 386.

49Ibid., p. 380.

50A. de Benoist, cited in Brunn, La Nouvelle Droite, p. 14.

51In Nouvelle école, no. 4, cited by M. Savary, L'Arche (Sept.-Oct., 1980).

52Nouvelle école (June, 1979), cited in Brunn, Nouvelle Droite, p. 138.

53Savary, L'Arche (Sept.-Oct., 1980).

54See Le Figaro-magazine, Feb. 10, 1979.

55Ibid.

56See Le Monde, Nov. 10, 1979.

57Brunn, La Nouvelle Droite, p. 331.

58S. Trigano, "C'est le juif qui est en question," Le Monde (Sept. 1, 1979).

59Le Monde, Oct. 15, 1980, p. 2.

60H. Asseo and P. Allard, "Ces messieurs de la Nouvelle Droite," Les Nouveaux cahiers, no. 56 (Spring, 1979), p. 11.

61Le Monde, Oct. 19, 1983.

62Présent, June 23, 1983, quoted in E. Plenel and A. Rollat, "The Revival of the Right in France," Patterns of Prejudice, Vol. 18, no. 2 (1984), p. 26.

63Cited in Plenel and Rollat, Patterns of Prejudice, p. 27.

64Le Monde, Oct. 19, 1983.

65Le Monde, Nov. 2, 1984.

66Information juive (October, 1984).

67Théo Klein quoted in Le Monde, Sept. 16, 1984.

# CHAPTER VII

# The Left: The New and The Old

If the anti-Jewish violence in the late 1970s and early 1980s was attributed primarily to the neo-Nazi right, the foundation for it was laid, since 1967, by the more influential and more numerous left. Some of the same Socialist forces, which earlier in the century were perceived by Jews as their protective shield, now embraced anti-Zionism, and at times voiced it in barely disguised anti-Semitic rhetoric. In the final days of the 1982 war in Lebanon, Bernard-Henri Lévy stated unequivocally: "we are witnessing a return of left-wing anti-Semitism."[1]

From the early 1970s, when anti-Zionism and government pro-Arab policy emerged as a serious concern to the Jewish community in France, it became obvious that one of the most adamant foes it had to contend with was a constellation of powerful forces on the left. Although not monolithic, and not uniformly hostile to the Jewish state, the entire left-of-center political spectrum contained elements inimical in varying degrees to Israel. After the rue Copernic explosion, Daniel Mayer, the former President of the French League of Human Rights, remarked on the hardships encountered by those who opposed the government's consistently pro-Arab policies which were generally supported by the left: "In France it is difficult to hold one's own and to oppose a political force that puts pressure on public opinion in the name of the Communists, leftists, and a non-Communist left."[2] Although not always united, the Communists — until the 1981 election consistently one of the largest parties in the country — segments of the Socialist Party, left-wing Gaullists and "progressive" Catholics formed a block hostile to Zionism. Commenting on the fact that the French Foreign Minister, Sauvagnargues, was the first major Western diplomat to shake hands with Yasser Arafat, a Jewish scholar suggested that, ironically, this significant political signal by a Minister in a conservative government was facilitated by support from the left. The French Foreign Minister "availed himself of a good progressive conscience in going to see Arafat."[3]

Along with the fight against colonialism in Algeria and Indochina, and opposition to the American involvement in Vietnam, the Palestinian cause has been a prominent issue for the French left. From the late 1960s on, at left-wing rallies, student demonstrations, and in leftist publications, Israel became synonymous with Fascism, colonialism and imperialism. The glorified image of the Palestinian "resistance fighter" replaced in leftist mythology the Algerian freedom-fighter. The Israeli soldier was portrayed as the reincarnated French paratrooper who had brutally repressed Arabs in North African casbahs. By 1970 it seemed that the young generation of leftists, which had missed out on the struggle against colonialism in Algeria in the 1950s, and the protests against the American involvement in Vietnam in the 1960s, had found its cause in anti-Zionism. Conveniently, like the Algerian peasant, the Palestinian was a Muslim who could be linked to the Third World. For the older generation, guilt over colonial misdeeds in Algeria could be expiated in the fight against "Zionist imperialism."

America's withdrawal from Vietnam resulted in an almost exclusive concentration on the Palestinian issue on French university campuses. In the 1970s, the various committees in support of the Vietcong were quickly transformed into committees for the P.L.O.; American "imperialism" became Zionist "imperialism." Few questioned the propriety of applying the standard leftist slogans to the Arab-Israeli conflict, of portraying Israel as merely a platform for American designs on the Middle East. There was no attempt to understand the historical and humanitarian factors behind Israel's existence and its struggle for survival.

This left-wing anti-Zionism served as a reminder that the birth of modern anti-Semitism in nineteenth-century France was more closely linked to Socialist ideologies than to their right-wing counterparts. Some Socialists were "not only infected with racism, but this racism was often intimately linked to their doctrines."[4] The logic of their thinking inevitably lead them to view the Jew as the "symbolic equivalent of all capitalist turpitudes."[5] If, through the centuries, the Jews aroused religious hatred, and the image of the wandering Jew elicited disdain mixed with pity, Alphonse de Toussenel, a Socialist follower of Fourier, was among the first to stress the Jews' dishonesty and disloyalty to the state.[6] Toussenel accused the Jew of using his statelessness as a vehicle for plotting "an international financial conspiracy."[7] This accusation was later to figure as a major element in *The Protocols of the Elders of Zion*, Toussenel's book also represented the first modern elaboration of the myth that the misery of the working classes stemmed primarily from the Jewish control of banks, trade and industry. Drumont, inspired by Toussenel, served as a link between left-wing and right-wing Catholic anti-Semitism.

Until the turn of the century, when the extreme-right took over the banner of anti-Semitism, other left-wing French ideologists exploited it as a political tool. The writings of Proudhon, Blanqui, Tridon, famous names in the history of French Socialism, reveal that their political denunciation of the Jew was also linked to a visceral hatred. Pierre-Joseph Proudhon, whose writings had considerable influence upon other Socialist thinkers, advocated that Jews be either sent "back to Asia or exterminated." He depicted the Jew as the enemy of the entire human race. Like Toussenel, Proudhon urged that anti-Semitism become an article of faith of Socialist ideology. Auguste Blanqui preached the view that the struggle against capitalism is synonymous with the battle against the Jew. He also labelled universal suffrage, which he strongly opposed, as a Jewish concept.[8] Gustave Tridon, a leading member of the Paris Commune, called for a fight against the "evil and satanic" Semitic race that strove to exploit the gentiles.[9] Jules Guesde, the man who introduced Marxist theory into the French Socialist movement, declared that the "true Republic" will come into existence only with the disappearance of the Rothschilds from French soil.[10]

It was another French thinker with Socialist leanings who influenced directly the thought of Adolf Hilter. Georges Vacher de Lapouge's book, *L'Aryen et son rôle social*[11], was carefully read by the Nazi leader and undoubtedly contributed to the development of his racist theories.[12] The French pseudo-scientist backed up his claims of Aryan superiority with "evidence" from research on skull measurements. The Jew, he wrote, was given to "parasitic life," he is "nothing but a predator."[13] The architects of Vichy's racial policies awarded Vacher de Lapouge a place of honor in their anti-Jewish propaganda campaign.

With the advent of right-wing anti-Semitism at the turn of the century, and with the growing trust placed by many Jews in Marxist ideology, the Jew-hatred of the early Socialists was almost forgotten. It was only in the 1960s, when anti-Zionism with its anti-Semitic overtones, became a slogan of the left that the history of Socialist anti-Semitism became the subject of renewed interest for historians seeking an explanation for what appeared as a remarkable paradox.

The transfer of the hostility toward Israel to French Jewry in the early 1970s was felt particularly in student circles. The defenders of Israel were labelled as agents of a colonial power. On the highly politicized university campuses Jewish students confronted with shouts of "Israël assassin," were either forced to hide their identity or to suffer verbal and physical abuse. By 1970, the situation aroused grave concerns. A student group protested against "cowardly attacks against Jewish students" and a "climate of anti-Semitic terror that is developing in French universities."[14]

The pro-Palestinian propaganda, echoed on both high-school and university campuses, created tension between Jewish and non-Jewish students. The situation was further aggravated by the presence in the ranks of the pro-Palestinians of significant numbers of alienated young Jews who often displayed particular anti-Israeli zeal in an effort to prove their "liberal" credentials. Even the more Jewishly committed students had to consider the fact that, unless they agreed to suppress their feelings of solidarity with Israel, they risked being excluded from the ranks of the popular leftist organizations which set the tone on the campuses.

The anti-Zionist slogans of the leftists, often echoed by leftist Gaullists, degenerated into traditional anti-Semitic insults. As a distinguished political scientist observed: the left's "constant attacks and accusations against Israel...prepared an anti-Semitic climate."[15] The writer, Pierre Goldman, a former Marxist student leader, recalled how pro-Palestinian campus discourse was often permeated with hatred towards Jews: "Some of us, leftist Jews, were held back from supporting the Palestinian cause by the unmistakable anti-Semitism that oozed from the pro-Palestinian speeches."[16] Perturbed by the anti-Semitism on the campuses, a leftist Jewish student group calling itself, "For the Recognition of Israel and Against Anti-Semitism," stated in a pamphlet: "anti-Zionist positions easily find an audience because of a long anti-Semitic tradition in Europe...the young often become aware of the Jewish problem through Arab propaganda."[17]

The well-organized machinery of the French Communist Party, with its high-circulation daily, L'Humanité, readily supported the Middle Eastern stand of the administrations of De Gaulle, Pompidou and Giscard d'Estaing. Major factions of the French Socialist Party also expressed strong support for the

Palestinians. Its pro-Communist, anti-American wing, the "CERES," led by the influential Jean-Pierre Chevènement, championed the Palestinian cause, and seldom condemned P.L.O. terrorism. By the very fact that they did not denounce anti-Israeli terrorism, while supporting the P.LO., the various leftist factions "stimulated anti-Jewish terror, lending it a sort of normality."[18]

The French Communist Party, the most staunchly Stalinist in Europe, backed Soviet hostility toward Israel just as it whitewashed anti-Semitic policies of the Soviet regime. In 1953, it mimicked Stalin's indignation over the "crimes" of Jewish doctors, who had allegedly plotted to assassinate the Soviet ruler, and saw to it that even the Paris-based Yiddish Communist daily, *Naie Presse*, also supported the accusations. The French Communists maintained silence over the Russian Jewry immigration issue, as well as on Polish anti-Semitism in the late 1960s. When a number of well-known intellectuals left the Party some of the Jews among them pointed out that anti-Semitism played an important role in their decision. Guy Konopnicki, the former head of "Jeunesses Communistes de France," a Communist youth movement, also cited the Party's hypocrisy in condemning anti-Semitism in France (its right-wing variety), while remaining silent about its existence in the U.S.S.R.[19]

Only days after De Gaulle's condemnation of Israel for "firing the first shot" in the Six Day War, *L'Humanité* published under the signature of an important member of the Party, an article in which a celebration at the liberated Western Wall in Jerusalem was compared to a satanic ceremony. "The presence of certain figures of high finance gave the ceremony a meaning that differed from religious fervor ... the spectacle recalled, as in *Faust*, that Satan led the ball. Even the golden calf was not missing ... as in Gounod's opera, lying at its feet in blood and mud, the result of its diabolical machinations." The author added that "he had information" about the presence at these "saturnalia" of two representatives of the "cosmopolitan tribe of bankers, well-known in all the countries of the world, Alain and Edmond de Rothschild."[20] When Georges Pompidou, a former banker, became Prime Minister in 1969, *L'Humanité* titled the story on its front page: "The director of the Rothschild Banks forms the government."[21] In vilifying "parasites" who "monopolize" French capital, the Communist daily cited only the names of two Jews, Rothschild and Dassault.[22]

During the May, 1968 student revolt the head of the Communist Party, Georges Marchais, drew attention to the fact that the student leader, Daniel Cohn-Bendit, was of Jewish origin. In an angry editorial against the students, many of whom claimed to espouse Maoist and anarchist ideologies his Party abhorred, Marchais labelled Cohn-Bendit as "that German anarchist." (Although educated in France he held German citizenship.) The euphemistic name-calling carried racist overtones and shocked many Jewish Communists, as Guy Konopnicki later revealed. In the revolutionary climate of the student rebellion Marchais reminded the frightened French public of the role played by German Jews in the revolutions of the nineteenth and twentieth centuries.

Already in 1970, in an article entitled "Are the French Racists?," Jean Lacouture noted the tendency to vent anti-Semitic sentiment under the guise of anti-Zionism. Racism, he wrote, was "strangely skillful in tacking itself on to new patterns," it was apt to give "an anti-Semitic coloration to a criticism of Zionism or of the State of Israel."[23] A historian remarked that the tactic of hiding anti-Semitism under the anti-Zionist label was practiced mainly by the left. The new historical juncture merely allowed the re-emergence of old ideological strains: "under the guise of anti-Zionism, the old anti-Semitism of the left, latent since the beginning of the century, resumed its march in a quickened pace."[24]

Shortly after General De Gaulle's angry condemnation of the Jewish state in 1967, left-wing Gaullists opened a sustained anti-Zionist campaign which stressed the argument that Israel was the main source of tension in the Middle East and that it created discord in French internal politics.[25] Some of the left-wing Gaullists denounced Zionist ideology for creating a dual loyalty problem, for its tendency to sway the Jews, a "universal people," to the side of "one particular state."[26] One left-wing Gaullist publication accused both Israel and Diaspora Jewry of fomenting a conspiracy. Israel, it claimed, has at its disposal "in every country where there are large Jewish communities unconditional allies ready to pressure their governments...and to condemn any government that does not yield to this pressure."[27] Some of De Gaulle's leftist supporters were apparently former members of anti-Semitic right-wing movements.[28]

Consistent anti-Zionist positions were echoed, from the late 1960s on, not only in L'Humanité, but also in the leftist daily Libération, and such leftist weeklies as Politique-Hebdo, La Cause du Peuple, Tout, Charlie-Hebdo and Témoignage Chrétien. In the words of a well-known publicist, since 1968 "Maoists and certain publications such as Témoignage Chrétien, have waged a sustained, blind and violent campaign against Israel. Most of the time it has been impossible to distinguish between attacks against Israel and those against Jews."[29] Paradoxically many of the left-wing publications, claiming a monopoly in the fight against all racisms, would, on occasion, also denounce anti-Semitism, especially when it could be pinned on their right-wing foes, or on the Jews themselves.

In a study of the coverage of the Yom Kippur War in *Libération*, Martine Cohen found that the "Zionism-Racism" formula was propagated by the leftist daily before the 1975 United Nations resolution that enshrined the purported validity of this concept.[30] *Libération* considered Israel to be the aggressor in the October, 1973, Syrian-Egyptian surprise attack. The daily also took a stand in support of Palestinian terrorism and used anti-Semitic clichés to criticize the Jewish state. In 1976, *Libération* considered the Israeli rescue mission of hostages held at Uganda's Entebbe airport as "an unwarranted interference in the affairs of a sovereign nation,"[31] and the newspaper's publisher, Serge July, entitled his editorial dealing with the remarkable rescue: "Israel: the Champion of Terrorism." *Libération* also viewed Israel as an agent of American imperialism in the Middle East, portraying the Palestinians as the oppressed Jews, and the Israelis as Nazis.

*Libération* illustrates the transformation of anti-Zionism into anti-Semitism. Cohen's study shows that *Libération* wrote, among other, that Israel is the "land of money," that French Jews, such as aircraft manufacturer Marcel Dassault (it ignored the fact that he was a convert to Christianity), were money-hungry merchants, and that Zionism is responsible for anti-Semitism. In a particularly invidious association of terms, recalling Nazi crimes against Jews, the leftist daily printed an article in which Zionists were accused of "deporting," Morrocan Jews to Israel in order to use them to "massacre" Palestinians.[32]

*Libération* also charged that Israelis practiced the same anti-Arab racism as the French colonialists in Algeria. Its pages echoed complaints that "Jews are everywhere" and suggestions that a world Jewish conspiracy does indeed exist. The language used in its columns was replete with "metaphors, metonymy and defective analyses" oozing Jew-hatred. The study of *Libération* concludes: "through theoretical arguments it attempts to justify... its wish for the destruction of the State of Israel, as the state of the Jews."[33] In its rejection of Christian guilt *Libération* rationalized a desire for the disappearance of the Jewish state in its new perception of the Israelis as "Jews who have surpassed the condition of the Jew as a victim."[34]

Left-wing French Catholicism has also played a significant role in spreading anti-Zionist propaganda, at times in the form of a reincarnation of theological anti-Semitism. Already in the pre-World War II years liberal Catholics, who seemed immune to racism, clustered around the journal *Esprit*, that displayed "an innocent form of French anti-Semitism."[35] Since 1967, the Catholic weekly, *Témoignage Chrétien*, has conducted a persistent campaign which combined a theological delegitimation of Israel with a New-Left critique of its social and military policies, and castigated the Jewish state in terms that could only imply a wish for its disappearance. Israel, Georges Montaron, the editor of the widely-circulated *Témoignage Chrétien* wrote, "represents a grave danger for all believers who read God's word in the Bible by maintaining a confusion between the sacred and the temporal, by its materialistic interpretation of the Bible and utilization of the Holy Books for a political purpose."[36] The Catholic weekly called its faithful to "fight Zionism, its racial character, its expansionist will." It also declared itself in "solidarity with the profound motivations of the Palestinian resistance,"[37] and coined a malicious historical metaphor: "Jesus was a Palestinian refugee."[38]

The anti-Zionism of this weekly, with its evangelical Marxism, was dangerous that it led "only too often to purely anti-Semitic attitudes."[39] Montaron waxed indignant over "disloyal" French Jews who supported Israel: "the network of accomplices the government of Tel Aviv relies on, the pressure groups...."[40] In May, 1970, he organized a conference of "Christians for Palestine" which blamed Israel and Zionist ideas for perpetuating the Middle East conflict. Held in Lebanon, the conference left little doubt in the minds of observers that it was motivated, in part, by traditional Christian anti-Semitism.

A contributor to *Témoignage Chrétien*, Father Paul Gauthier, invented a new charge against the Jews that suited post-war geo-political divisions in the world. Alluding to world Jewry's support for Israel the French cleric asked: "Where do the dollars sent by American and other Jews to Israel come from? Is it not from the exploitation of under-developed nations still held in economic slavery?"[41] This charge added a new element to the compendium of anti-Jewish canards: the Jew has also become the exploiter of Third World countries in Asia and Africa. During the 1982 war in Lebanon *Témoignage Chrétien* compared Palestinian terrorists, who in their raids deliberately targeted Jewish children, to the Warsaw Ghetto fighters.

The Jewish cause in France has also been harmed by the fact that some in the leftist Jewish intelligentsia have participated in the anti-Zionist campaigns. Still clinging to the old belief that the triumph of the left will solve the "Jewish problem," and driven by a misguided idealism, a number of Jewish intellectuals joined the chorus of Israel's detractors. The presence of Jews in its ranks conveniently absolved the left of accusations of anti-Semitism, and helped it to divert the blame for the upsurge of Jew-hatred on the less numerous, and relatively less significant, anti-Semitic right. Many Jews were reluctant to give up the notion that the left was their ally: "a long historical experience...has developed among Jews a kind of conditioned reflex: any anti-Semitic aggression was automatically attributed to the right, while the left was viewed, blindly, as a permanently open, hospitable refuge."[42]

At least two generations of French Jews grew up with the belief that Socialism, in its various stripes, represented a protective shield against anti-Semitism and a vehicle for integration into French society. The Socialist call for brotherhood, for unity of "proletarians of all nations," and for social justice, captivated the imagination of thousands of young Jews who succumbed to the temptation of an ideology that promised dignity and equality, and an end to centuries of persecution to the downtrodden people.

In the 1930s the young Eastern European Jewish immigrants to France found that the shortest path to assimilation into French society led through the Communist Party. Becoming part of the Communist milieu, with its rituals and customs, was the quickest way of entering French life. Although the promised fraternity eventually proved to be an illusion, many would continue to embrace the fiction of Marxist "brotherly solidarity." Few had the insight to realize that loyalty to party ideology would exact the heavy price of denial of their ethnic and religious identity in exchange for a social acceptance that was never whole-hearted. A former Jewish Communist complained that the PCF has room for Jews only when they are "sterilized," when they consent to suppress their Jewish consciousness. He called those who remained in the Party "Juifs honteux" (sheepish Jews).

A prominent student of French Communism has written that several generations of French Jews have fallen to the temptation of joining the ranks of the left in an effort "to break the link of chosenness and of exile."[43] To remove the suspicion that he was "different," the Jew had to refrain from showing any particularism by adopting a universalist outlook. Later, many Jews were reluctant to face the betrayal of their trust and viewed Communism's hostility to Judaism as a "temporary, inconsequential regression which was ignored or interpreted, against all evidence, in a manner favorable to the left."[44]

This blind loyalty was also dictated by the highly monolithic nature of French society, which intensified the desire for acceptance among minority groups. Until recently, a chauvinistic, Jacobin mentality has tended to marginalize those who were not considered fully French, particularly Jews. The left, on the other hand, with its promises to abolish religious and national barriers, tantalized many Jews through "an idealistic, almost mystical impulse."[45] By proving their loyalty to "progressive" ideals the Jews hoped to prove that they were worthy of becoming part of French society, or at least part of the French "Socialist family", which seemed less bent on rejecting them.

To demonstrate their "liberalism" some Jews went as far as to voice opinions that were plainly anti-Semitic. In 1972, a Jew identified as a "leftist Gaullist", attacked Zionism in terms that distorted history and insulted the memory of Jewish martyrs. Zionism, he argued, "is a separatist movement for Jews, just as in the nineteenth century Ultramontanism was for the Catholics; both are clerical. Zionism is a crusade, and any crusade, whether in the name of the cross or of the Star of David, is blameworthy."[46] The comparison of Zionism with the fanatic Crusaders who slaughtered innocent Jews in the name of religion, verged on self-hatred. Another Jew, a professor of literature, claimed in Le Monde that Zionism was "basically a mystic and chauvinistic ideology that is morally totalitarian."[47] The same individuals who denied the right of self-determination to their own people were eagerly supporting that right for the Palestinians.

While highly regarded orientalists argued that Israel's 1976 victory over the Arabs represented a return to colonialism,[48] Maxime Rodinson, a specialist on Islam and a staunch advocate of the Arab cause, characterized Israel as a "cyst" in the Arab world and viewed as "mythical" the Jewish claim to the Holy Land.[49] Shortly before the Six Day War he wrote that the creation of the State of Israel on Palestinian land conformed to Western colonial practices which strove to achieve economic domination of the natives. The fact that Rodinson was of Jewish origin and a prominent orientalist, heartened Israel's detractors. Rodinson typifies, wrote the author of a book on left-wing anti-Zionism, those

Jewish intellectuals...who wish to ignore Judaism, as well as their own link to it."[50] For another Communist Jew, André Wurmser, Jews who demonstrated their support for Israel during the Six Day War "were stricken with madness and didn't act like loyal Frenchmen."[51] Because of their "excessive interest" in Israel, he added, Jews are justly accused of dual loyalty.[52] A writer, describing himself as a "free Jew," argued that "the subservience of Jews to the State of Israel is the most powerful anti-Semitic factor engendered by Jews in four thousand years."[53]

In the spring of 1980, a group calling itself "Jews of the Left", issued a "manifesto"[54] which condemned Israel for a variety of "sins." In terms that implicitly suggested that Israel is a dictatorial power imposing its domination on all Jews, the "Juifs de Gauche" proclaimed their "rejection of any Jewish centrality and of all obedience toward Jerusalem or the Zionist movement." The word "obedience" conjured up images well-entrenched in the popular French anti-Semitic imagination: Jews, dispersed through the world, constitute a fifth column that is under the total control of a mighty, malevolent clique based in Jerusalem. The "manifesto" also called for negotiations with the P.L.O. "in order to satisfy Palestinian national aspirations," without demanding that the terrorist organization recognize Israel's right to exist or that it renounce a clause in its "covenant" pledging to destroy it.

Among the signatories of the "manifesto" was Pierre Vidal-Naquet, a historian, who had been for many years a consistent critic of Israel, espousing anti-Zionist and pro-Palestinian notions which he often expressed in the pages of Le Monde. Typical of a certain assimilated Jewish-French milieu, Vidal-Naquet personifies those who, in the name of liberalism and universalist ideas, use their tenuous Jewish identity to castigate their fellow Jews for not living up to the highest standards of morality. Léon Poliakov, the historian of anti-Semitism, wrote that Vidal-Naquet was among those who, since June 1967, "declared war" against Zionism "in the name of humanism."[55] At the outbreak of the 1982 war in Lebanon Vidal-Naquet compared Prime Minister Begin's reference to the shooting of the Israeli Ambassador to Great Britain as one of the P.L.O.'s crimes, to Hitler's pretexts for instigating the Crystal Night pogroms.

Another signatory of the 1980 leftist Jews' "manifesto" was Wladimir Rabi. A longtime activist who defended Jewish causes in the 1930s and in the post-war period, Rabi became after the Six Day War an unrelenting critic of the State of Israel because, in his eyes, it did not live up to the eternal values of Judaism and no longer served as a "light to the nations." A frequent contributor to *Le Monde*, he attacked prominent Jewish figures in France who represented the hated "Zionist establishment" (he claimed that he was forced to criticize Jews in *Le Monde* because he was "censored" in the Jewish press). Rabi also turned into a virulent critic of anyone not joining him in condemning alleged torture in Israel. Although he admitted, in his last book, that systematic torture did not exist in the Jewish state, he chastized French Jewish intellectuals for not supporting his flimsily documented allegations.[56] His passion for his own definition of justice led Rabi to attribute such totalitarian practices as Stalinism, censorship and the "perversion" of language to French Jewish thinkers and to the Jewish "establishment." Such distinguished Jewish intellectuals as Raymond Aron, Vladimir Jankélevitch, Emmanuel Lévinas, Arnold Mandel and Annie Kriegel were castigated by Rabi for their stand in defense of Israel and Zionism. Self-righteously, he characterized Jewish "master thinkers" as "hypocrites" seized by "folly, hysteria and delirium," and wrote that the defenders of Israel were guilty of "flattery and charlatanism."[57]

The 1980 "manifesto", one of several issued periodically by similar "progressive" Jewish groups, highlighted the fact that in France, as in no other major Jewish Diaspora, the Jewish community, though overwhelmingly supportive of Israel, has had to contend with significant elements in its midst which tended to support the propaganda emanating from anti-Zionist quarters. Thus, in addition to the struggle against the government's pro-Arab policies, against those who accused if of double loyalty and against anti-Semites on the left and on the right, beleaguered French Jewry has also had to ward off enemies from within. The foes of Judaism were only too delighted to see a number of Jewish intellectuals "join . . . the camp of their enemies."[58] The attacks of these highly assimilated Jews, lacking a profound understanding of the Jewish ethos, have no doubt contributed to weakening the entire community.

The fight against anti-Semitism in France has also suffered from the largely passive attitude adopted by the large and influential intelligentsia that identifies generally with the left. In a country where intellectual debate on social and political issues is highly developed, and entrenched in an old tradition, issues pertaining to the anti-Jewish manifestations have been largely ignored by the same circles that invariably spring to the defence of the human

rights of any social, racial, or ethnic constituency. The conspicuous militant left-wing Catholics, who often voice their opposition
to injustice and discrimination, remained silent in the face of the
new Judeophobia. Reacting to the flare-up of anti-Semitic rhetoric in the summer of 1982, including the left-wing Christian
publications, and the silence from the Church leadership that
greeted it, a French-Jewish academic wrote: "the lack of reaction
on the part of the Christians is...an extremely disturbing fact."[59]

Already in 1969, the sociologist Edgar Morin noted the absence
of reaction among intellectuals in Orléans to an anti-Semitic
rumor that almost resulted in a pogrom against the town's Jewish
shopkeepers. Incited by a fictitious report about abduction and
white slavery which circulated in a Catholic girl's school, a story
alleging that several young women had disappeared after entering clothing stores owned by Jews, an angry crowd gathered
intent on taking the law into its hands. Disaster was prevented at
the last moment. The author of La Rumeur d'Orléans "was struck
the most by the failure of the teachers to intercede with the
students and the town's population at the moment the rumor was
in a stage of incubation, as well as later when it had spread."[60] The
fact that the professors of the local university had remained on
the sidelines was also "a sign of inertia."[61]

Léon Poliakov suggested that the apathy of the Orléans intellectuals was due to the presence in the town's leftist university
circles, as in most other French universities, of a pro-Arabism
which inhibited action against the threat to Jews.[62] The "traditional" foes of racism had failed an important test. Unfortunately,
this was not to be the last time. The anti-Semitism in the media
and on the streets during the summer months of 1982 was the
result of an accumulation of fifteen years of left-wing "anti-
Zionist", rhetoric that had by then managed to permeate the
lexicon of political discourse in France.

France also became one of the few Western democracies where
local, extreme-left terrorists, specifically targeted Jews. It is also
one of the few Western countries where evidence presented to a
court has shown that leftist terrorists attacked Jewish targets
independently from their Palestinian allies. In June, 1983, at his
trial in Paris, a leader of "Action Directe," a violent Marxist
organization accused of bombing several Jewish and Israeli estab-
lishments, declared that Israel was a "Fascist" state, a "bunker of
Western capitalism," and that it was a "duty" to contribute to the
"total destruction of this state."[63] Frédéric Oriach, the head of the

143

terrorist gang and several of his cohorts were convicted to prison terms ranging from six years to eight months. The court was presented with evidence that the group had planned to attack thirty-eight "Zionist" targets in Paris — in fact, local communal leaders and institutions. In France, extreme-leftists imitated the fanaticism of Palestinian radicals.

# Notes

[1]*Le Monde*, Sept. 9, 1982.

[2]*L'Arche*, Nov., 1980, p. 32.

[3]J. Tarnero, *L'Arche* (Sept.-Oct., 1979).

[4]Lévy, *L'Idéologie française*, p. 31.

[5]*Ibid.*

[6]Alphonse de Toussenel, *Les Juifs rois de l'époque, histoire de la féodalité financière* (Paris: Librairie de l'Ecole Sociétaire, 1845). See Paul Bénichou's concise analysis of some of Toussenel's "innovations" in "Sur quelques sources françaises de l'antisémitisme moderne," *Commentaire*, no. 1 (1978), pp. 67-79.

[7]Bénichou, *Commentaire*, p. 71.

[8]Sternhell, *La Droite révolutionnaire*, p. 189.

[9]*Ibid.*, p. 191.

[10]Lévy, *L'Idéologie française*, pp. 127-128.

[11]Paris: Albert Fontemoing, 1899.

[12]Lévy, *L'Idéologie française*, p. 130.

[13]*L'Aryen*, p. 471.

[14]*Le Monde*, Jan. 21, 1970.

[15]J. Ellul, *Le Monde*, Oct. 15, 1980.

[16]*Libération*, Oct. 31, 1978.

[17]From a May, 1970 pamphlet published by C.A.R.I.C.A., a student group "For the Recognition of Israel and Against Anti-Semitism."

[18]A. Mandel, *Le quotidien de Paris*, Oct. 9, 1980.

[19]*Le Matin*, Nov. 4, 1978.

[20]Benoît Franchon, *L'Humanité*, June 17, 1967.

[21]Cited in Lévy, *L'Idéologie française*, p. 280.

[22]*Ibid.*

[23]*Le Monde*, March 20, 1970.

[24]H. Arvon, *Les Juifs et l'idéologie* (Paris: PUF, 1978), p. 124.

[25]Cohen, *De Gaulle*, p. 277.

[26]*Ibid.*

[27]*La Nation*, Jan. 21, 1970, cited by Cohen, *De Gaulle*, p. 280.

[28]Cohen, *De Gaulle*, pp. 286-87.

[29]J. Bloch-Michel, *Dissent* (Summer, 1980), p. 292.

[30]M. Cohen, "Le Quotidien *Libération* et la guerre du Kippour," *Les Temps modernes* (May, 1978), pp. 1817-1864.

[31]Cited by Bloch-Michel, *Dissent*, p. 292.

[32]Cohen, *Les Temps modernes* (May, 1978), p. 1849.

[33]*Ibid.*, p. 1864.

[34]*Ibid.*

[35]B.-H. Lévy, *L'Arche* (February, 1981). For a while, during the Vichy period, *Espirit* favored collaboration with Pétain's Fascist state. See B.-H. Lévy, *L'idéologie française*, p. 48.

[36]Cited in *Le Monde*, Dec. 19, 1969.

[37]*Ibid.*

[38]Cited by J. Tarnero, "Le Refoulé est de retour," *Les Nouveaux cahiers*, no. 56 (Spring, 1979), p. 8.

[39]Y. Chevalier, *L'Arche* (Sept.-Oct., 1979).

[40]G. Montaron, quoted in *Le Monde*, Jan. 4-5, 1970.

[41]Cited in Givet, *La Gauche contre Israël*, p. 138.

[42]Arvon, *Les Juifs et l'idéologie*, p. 145.

[43]A. Kriegel, *Communismes au miroir français* (Paris: Gallimard, 1974), p. 220.

[44]Arvon, *Les Juifs et l'idéologie*, p. 122.

[45]Mandel, *Nous autres Juifs*, p. 261.

[46]B. Bettelheim, *Le Monde*, Dec. 1, 1972. Cited in Cohen, *De Gaulle*, p. 280.

[47]R. Cohen, *Le Monde*, Dec. 21-22, 1969.

[48]Jacques Berque cited by Givet, *La Gauche contre Israël*, pp. 42-43.

[49]Givet, *La Gauche contre Israël*, pp. 46-47.

[50]*Ibid.*, p. 150.

[51]*Fidèlement votre* (Paris: Grasset, 1979), p. 484. This André Wurmser is not to be confused with his namesake, an official of the Jewish community.

[52]*Ibid.*

[53]M. Rachline, *Un Juif libre* (Paris: Guy Authier, 1976), p. 227.

[54]Published in *Le Monde* on March 29, 1980.

[55]L. Poliakov, *De l'antisionisme à l'antisémitisme*, p. 160.

[56]*Un Peuple de trop sur la terre.*

[57]*Ibid.*, pp. 69, 21, 17.

[58]Givet, *La Gauche contre Israël*, p. 194.

[59]D. Lindenberg, "Dérapage de la gauche?," *Les Nouveaux cahiers*, no. 71, p. 15.

[60]Edgar Morin, *La Rumeur d'Orléans* (Paris: Seuil, 1969), p. 84.

[61]*Ibid.*, p. 85.

[62]*Ibid.*, p. 86.

[63]*Le Monde*, June 18, 1983.

# CHAPTER VIII

# A Community Under Pressure

"It was not, and it is not, the easiest of fates to be a French Jew," wrote a keen observer of the Jewish scene in France.[1] From the time of his emancipation in the eighteenth century the French Jew has had to face powerful homogenizing forces in a highly monolithic society in his struggle to preserve his heritage. According to the Constituent Assembly's Law of Emancipation of 1791, Jewish identity was to be maintained only as a private "conscience" limited in its public expression to religious worship. As time would show, the assimilationist aspect of the historic law had the effect of stifling both religious commitment and the concept of Jewish nationhood among French Jewry.

The intent of the drafters of the law of emancipation was to eradicate Jewish culture, to assimilate the Jew into French society, in fact to convert him into a Frenchman exempted from Christian worship. By negating most phenomenological aspects of existential Judaism, except for confessional practice in a synagogue placed under the tutelage of the state, the framers of the law aimed to convert the Jew from a member in a corporate entity to a private figure. This was the real meaning of the famous phrase uttered at the 1789-1791 Constituent Assembly by the author of the law, Count Stanislas de Clermont-Tonnerre: "we must refuse everything to the Jews as a nation and grant them everything as individuals."

Another champion of emancipation, the Abbé Grégoire, saw the new law as a means that could facilitate the conversion of the Jews to Christianty. He argued that granting Jews their rights as citizens was one of the "most efficient methods of bringing them to our faith."[2] Still another rationale of the advocates of the law of emancipation was to bolster the Revolutionary credo, to gain greater acceptance for its constitution which proclaimed the equality of all citizens. In the effort to strengthen the unity of post-Revolutionary France the Jew was to serve as a model of the new experiment, to demonstrate the triumph of the Revolutionary ideas at a time when they were being opposed by significant segments of French society. Even the advocacy of freedom of conscience seems to have been a strategy to keep Jews from maintaining their unity as a nation. According to the author of a recent analysis of the law of emancipation the "generosity" of the Revolution was "full of demons."[3]

The law of emancipation soon bore fruit that fully justified the expectations of its framers. The "Israélite," as the assimilation-bound French Jew came to be called, was eager to adopt the ways of the Frenchman and to drop many of the tenets of traditional Judaism. French Jews proclaimed the French Revolution the greatest event in Jewish history since the Exodus from Egypt and France a second Promised Land. The Revolution succeeded in taking Israel out of the "Israélite." By the end of the century, French Jewry's communal solidarity, a traditional measure of commitment to Judaism, had weakened to the point that the community as a whole failed to take a stand in defense of Captain Dreyfus. It comes as no surprise that until recently critics of French Jewry have charged it with "assimilation so profound and destructive as to constitute self-delusion at best, moral cowardice at worst."[4]

By the late 1970s, however, most French Jews had concluded that the goal of assimilation was a tragic error.[5] Events in the 1970s created an awareness that proclamations of loyalty to France would not provide protection from verbal and physical threats. A growing number of French Jews, including some from the older, assimilated generation, came to the realization that in any upsurge of anti-Jewish violence they would have to share the sorrow with their brethren. Even the "neo-assimilated" Jews, a recent study shows, "no longer deny that anti-Semitism exists... no longer believe that anti-Semitism is a prejudice belonging to the remote past and destined to disappear in enlightened France."[6] After the rue Copernic synagogue bombing newspapers published articles by members of this liberal congregation, fully integrated into French society, who were asking themselves if they should be "packing their suitcase." As one of them wrote, "if it could happen in an assimilation-prone Liberal [Reform] synagogue, it could happen anywhere." Some expressed the painful dilemma in uncharacteristically frank terms: "I am through with living in the 'French-Jewish' consensus. But what can be done? Leave for Israel? Remain in France and fight, but how? ... Try to forget and to forgive? This would amount to betrayal."[7]

The re-examination of the Vichy period, especially following the turmoil created by the interview in *L'Express* with Darquier de Pellepoix, has reminded those who had forgotten, and has reinforced in the minds of those who did not, that many of the same French policemen who carried out the roundup of the Jews in 1942 and 1943 were still alive, that only a handful were punished, and that history can conceivably repeat itself. The anti-Jewish agitation was an indication in the minds of many Jews that the troubled relationship between them and their country would not be solved by declarations of undivided loyalty to the tricolor. The renewed hostility strengthened the belief that attempts to prove one's patriotism or universalism, to renounce what was scornfully called in the past "parochialism," would not do away with the verbal and physical attacks and would provide little protection against accusations of double loyalty. As a former Marxist intellectual put it succinctly: "We realized that we have lived too long in a state of schizophrenia, in the impossible ubiquity of a situation in which one keeps one foot here and one foot there, one in what was left of our repressed, ashamed Jewishness, and the other in an illusory universality called 'francité' [Frenchness] or internationalism."[8]

An echo of the new mentality was provided by the president of the "Fonds Social Juif Unifié," Baron Guy de Rothschild, who represented the same leadership that had been severely criticized by the younger generation for its low-key approach to crises and for its timidity. Three weeks after the explosion at the rue Copernic synagogue in October, 1980, Baron Rothschild stated that Jews will never again fall into a state of "inferiority, submission and fear" and that they will react to hostility with a combative hostility of their own.[9] Rothschild's statement came close to echoing the views of the militant young activists. It reflected a boldness pointedly absent from his previous statements. It showed a radical evolution in the mentality of the French-Jewish leadership, which was marked in the past by extreme self-doubt and timidity.

In April 1980, at a mass pro-Israel rally in Paris, the leader of a new militant Jewish movement called for the adoption of a strategy that represented a major departure from tradition: a break in the old, unwritten prohibition against Jewish block-voting and organizing the community as a political entity. The "Renouveau Juif" ("Jewish Renewal") movement considered itself as the spokesman of the new militant Jewish assertiveness which, among other points claimed the right to maintain close ties with other Jewish Diasporas, and above all, to express steadfast support for the State of Israel, even when such support clashed with government policy. The movement's leader, Henri Hajdenberg, told an interviewer: "French Jews must get over Ashkenazi fears that they won't be French if they proclaim their Jewishness."[10]

"Renouveau Juif" also accused the leaders of Jewish organizations of stifling and paralyzing authentic popular aspirations. At a 1980 rally he called "12 Hours for Israel," Hajdenberg charged the traditional leadership with "many weaknesses," "political bankruptcy" and encouraging assimilation. He urged the 150,000 Jews gathered at the outskirts of Paris to constitute themselves into an electoral pressure group, and to "sanction" the French government for its pro-Arab policies. The "Renouveau Juif" campaign showed that for the first time in their modern history, French Jews were not afraid to express their Jewish "particularism" and were shedding some of their old complexes. There was a growing sentiment that the Jewish masses wanted a leadership that was closer to their thinking and that it was time to change the old guard, the traditional "notables" who had headed the community for a century.[11]

While discouraging the creation of a "Jewish Lobby" on the American model, considered "alien" to French traditions (Raymond Aron and the former Minister Léo Hamon were among those who opposed open political activism), the leaders of the community seemed to be moving closer to the young militants. A few weeks before the 1980 "Renouveau Juif" mass rally, CRIF called on Jews "to mobilize against any political project favoring the Arab 'Rejectionist' camp at the expense of the vital interests of Israel."[12]

Until the early 1970s, French Jews generally avoided challenging government policy and expressed Jewish aspirations in general terms. In 1973, however, the leaders of the community asked the French authorities to intervene on behalf of Soviet Jewry and in 1977 CRIF issued a "manifesto" delineating Jewish concerns, including its steadfast commitment to the State of Israel.[13] There was also a reaction to the release by the French authorities of the alleged mastermind of the murder of the Israeli athletes at the Munich Olympics. The call by "Renouveau Juif" for direct political action was, however, a new step. A student of French Jewry has noted with surprise in 1980 that "the view that militancy is the normal and even the desirable form of Judaism is today not only shared by a majority of French Jews but is fundamental to the thinking of a number of writers."[14]

The new political activism also contrasted with French Jewry's earlier coolness to Zionism and the State of Israel. The creation of the Jewish state in 1948 did not seem to stir the imagination of the community. When the fledgling state was besieged by several Arab armies French Jewry followed the events with a relative lack of passion. During a solidarity meeting at the Wagram Hall in Paris in June, 1948, the seats remained two-thirds empty. There seemed to be little Jewish pressure on the French government which took seven months to recognize Israel's existence, and then only on a "de facto" basis. A similar indifference characterized the reaction to the 1956 Sinai campaign. It took the dramatic victory of the Six Day War to cause a marked change in both French Jewry's attitude to Israel and in its self-awareness as an ethnic group.

Israel's stunning 1967 military victory must be viewed as the most important factor that stimulated the process of change. In a country where the ugly image of the Jew has been nurtured for generations by some of the greatest literary figures, where abject anti-Semitic canards were repeatedly used as a political vehicle, where the word "Juif" has been synonymous with unmistakable stigma, the echo of the Israeli victory reverberated with magnified force. Its effect in erasing deeply ingrained stereotypes and in creating a liberating spirit can hardly be over-estimated. The dramatic reversal of the image of the cowardly Jew was enhanced by its contrast with the humiliating setbacks suffered by the French military in Indo-China and Algeria, the shame of the 1940 "drôle de guerre" and Vichy period.

Egypt's military moves and pledges to destroy Israel in the weeks prior to the outbreak of the 1967 war affected even the most assimilated Jews. The threat of another genocide that hovered over the Israelis in the weeks prior to the Six Day War induced despair and strengthened the bonds of solidarity. It also created, for the first time, a link between the marginal and the more committed segments of the Jewish community. In a few days in June, 1967 French Jews raised close to twelve million dollars for Israel, a sum equal to the total collected over the previous fifteen-year period. The Six Day War revealed an unsuspected depth of Jewish identity.

The close identification of French Jewry with Israel since 1967 has been repeatedly documented. Today, for almost the entire community the Jewish state represents a fundamental, if not exclusive, dimension of Jewish identity. This attachment cuts across all social, economic and religious segments of the community. Israel has become "the point of coalescence in which different ideas about the meaning of belonging to a Jewish community are combined into a single idea."[15] For some, according to the sociologist, Emeric Deutsch, the attachment to Israel is based on the Biblical promise; for others, Israel has created "the possibility of declaring one's Jewishness with pride . . . For almost all it is a fundamental dimension, if not the only one, of their Jewish identity."[16] Israel also evokes feelings of solidarity and admiration. According to the editor of Le Nouvel observateur, Jean Daniel, French Jewry "has contracted a debt toward Israel, because it has taught French Jews to confront misfortune and to fight standing up."[17] French Jews have "interiorized" the new enhanced image of the Jew created by the State of Israel. They have "drawn from the Israeli bravado a culture of affirmation."[18]

The example of Israeli steadfastness and assertiveness has also been transmitted by the many young French Jews who had a direct experience of Israeli life. While only a fraction of American Jewry has visited Israel, a far greater proportion of French Jews has done so. Among the youth, an even larger segment has either spent vacations in Israel or has worked on a kibbutz. The number of Jews from France studying in Israeli universities has been higher than that of any other Western country. The Israeli experience has no doubt affected the attitudes of many among them.

The transformation of French Jewry was also affected by the massive immigration, beginning in 1962, of Jews from the Maghreb. The North African Jews brought with them a degree of French culture and adjusted quickly to their new environment. Proud, assertive, attached to tradition, only indirectly affected by the trauma of the Holocaust, they stimulated communal life on every level. The increase in numerical strength and the geographic spread they provided had a positive effect on the community's image of itself.[19] It is the lower-middle-class segment among them, the majority, that is mainly responsible for the "reethnicization" of French Jewry.[20] A 1980 survey indicated that among those strongly committed to the preservation of Judaism 70% were Sephardim.[21] Only a minority among them has completely abandoned tradition. The absence of a significant linguistic and cultural barrier facilitated rapid integration and diminished the strains on their Jewish heritage, in contrast to the difficulties experienced by earlier, East European Jewish immigrations.

Spurring on the return to Jewish sources were several young writers of North African origin, the most prominent among them being Bernard-Henri Lévy and Shmuel Trigano. For the first time since emancipation Jewish writers who commanded the attention of a wide reading public presented Judaism not merely as an echo of the Western, Christian ethic, but as a source of Western civilization whose message has been diluted and distorted by Christianity. In his best-selling *Le Testament de Dieu*, Lévy portrayed Jewish monotheism as a political ethic capable of countering modern totalitarianisms. Trigano argued, in his three books, *Le Récit de la disparue*, *La Nouvelle question juive* and *Les Juifs et la République)* that emancipation has led to the Jew's alienation from his identity. He called for a return to traditional Jewish sources so that Jews could re-enter history on their own ethical foundation and not on that of concepts borrowed from non-Jewish thinkers.

Another major factor which contributed to the renewal of interest in Judaism was the decline in the late 1970s in the appeal of left-wing and universalist ideologies. Young Jews who had developed their social consciousness in the ranks of Marxist political movements inimical to Judaism now turned to Judaic studies and sought meaning in a forgotten heritage. In the face of cultural crisis, socio-economic changes and a blurring of the meaning of values the quest for Jewish identity filled a need that soon turned into an intellectual fashion. A member of a Paris study-group engaged in the rediscovery of Judaism through an immersion in traditional Jewish texts summarized the motivation for the new interest: "Feeling exiled from ideologies, loaded with a heavy university baggage, estranged from Judaism, we realized that there was an enormous gap [in our culture], and that Western civilization has buried our roots. We are now convinced that there is a Jewish civilization that is vital to our very existence and that has been ignored by the West since the time of the Greeks."[22]

Jewish revival in France and the psychological boldness that spurred it on was also affected by the emergence of militant regionalist sentiment. In the 1970s, for the first time since Richelieu, the monolithic, centralist structure of French society was beginning to crumble. In 1977, President Giscard d'Estaing declared that there no longer existed a contradiction between the aspiration to be considered a full-fledged French citizen and the desire to perpetuate one's ancestral traditions. The French President thereby officially sanctioned a new ethnic slogan, "le droit à la différence" ("The Right to be Different").

François Mitterrand's abolition of the traditional dominant authority of the Prefects was further evidence that, for the first time in modern history, the French government was ready to respond to the demands for greater political and cultural autonomy. The militancy of the Corsican separatists and the Breton autonomists, the quest for "Celtitude" and "Occitanisme," have stimulated Jewish claims to the right to affirm a national ethos within a context of civic equality. The valorisation of ethnic cultures has reinforced the revival of a more authentic Jewish conciousness.[23] In 1980, the editorialist of the Jewish monthly L'Arche stated: "The long-sought right to be different has almost been recognized."[24]

However, this optimistic assessment was not unanimous. In June, 1981 a prominent figure in French public life complained that there was a "secret limit" on Jews in French politics.[25] There were still obstacles to a Jew serving as Prime Minister or even as Foreign Minister. There were also serious limitations on a Jew who wished to be both a political activist and a militant Jew. There were many Jewish lawyers but only one Jewish President of the Bar (Bâtonnier). A senior official of CRIF claimed that Jews remain "marginal" in French society, that the community is still considered "foreign."[26] The plan to organize a Jewish vote was not only perceived as alien to the French political process but also as ammunition for the anti-Semites even by staunch friends of the Jewish community. In 1981, both the homogenizing and anti-Semitic fabric of French society were still sufficiently strong to deny Jews the full right to express their socio-political aspirations. It is quite evident that to be a Jew in France is still not comparable to being an Auvergnat or a Breton. Reflecting an old, timorous mentality, some Jews continued to believe that anti-Semitism should only be fought in the name of all racisms.[27]

The setbacks and frustrations engendered by the confrontations over France's pro-Arab policies in the 1970s have aroused in the minds of many the feeling that the French government's indifference to the fate of the State of Israel is linked to similar attitudes toward Jews during the Vichy period. The anti-Semitism from the left and the right, the legitimation of anti-Zionism, the government-sponsored anti-Israeli propaganda, convinced even the optimists that the "Jewish condition" was far from settled. It also brought with it the realization that the timid responses of the past, the attempts to escape, to hide from Jewishness, were based on a flawed premise, and that anti-Semites do not differentiate between committed and assimilated Jews.

François Debré, the son of the former Prime Minister, Michel Debré, echoed this feeling: "Jews try to assimilate in vain; there are always some individuals to remind them of their origin. I am only 25% Jewish but this fact does not prevent people from considering me as a Jew."[28] A similar sentiment was echoed by a man who became a cabinet minister in 1981: "life has proven to me that if one forgets that one is Jewish, others [non-Jews] do not."[29] For a prominent writer the experience of "the last two centuries has shown that timidity and assimilation" do not prevent hostility to Jews.[30] French Jews have reached the conclusion that "whether they are militant or not, ashamed of being Jewish or not, the anti-Semites will not ignore them."[31]

The renewal of interest in Judaism was no doubt stimulated by this realization. There emerged a collective Jewish awareness and a quest to re-acquire the Jewish heritage unparalleled in any other Diaspora in the last generation. "It has become natural to accept one's Jewishness," wrote the authors of the investigative reportage, *Juifs et Français.*[32] "There are no more sheepish Jews ['Juifs honteux'] in France," declared a well-known Jewish personality at a public meeting in Paris in June, 1981. The majority of French Jews "now wish to assume , in one form or another, a distinctive Jewish identity."[33] Pierre Dreyfus, the former President of the Régie Renault who became the Minister of Industry in the Mitterrand administration, stated that if in the past he felt 100% French, he now identified more with his Jewish heritage. This "Israélite," with old roots in France, expressed regret for not having been exposed to "the kind of Jewish culture people rediscover today."[34] "Returning [to Judaism] has become as acceptable as leaving it," according to Simon Schwarzfuchs.[35] Even more significantly, "the political dimension of the Jewish problem" has led some Jews to find their way back to cultural and religious Judaism.[36]

The scope of Jewish educational activities includes day schools, Talmud Torahs (elementary schools limited to religious instruction), courses for adults on the Talmud, Cabala, Yiddish and Ladino. University Jewish studies have attracted thousands of students. There has emerged a renewed interest in religion in what was an overwhelmingly secularized society. Jewish community centers, a relatively recent phenomenon in France, organized debates, lectures, and conferences on various aspects of Judaism and current Jewish concerns. *L'Express* commented on this startling phenomenon: "Fifty years ago they dreamt of disappearing as Jews; today it is the opposite."[37]

Former Marxists — dejected, like many French leftists, by the discovery of Stalin's Gulags and such Communist atrocities as those of the Pol Pot regime in Cambodia — turned to Judaism and engaged in Talmudic studies with the same vigour with which they had debated political ideology just a few years earlier. A young woman interviewed in a Paris Jewish community centre about the reasons for her participation in Jewish activities commented: "I never came here before, my parents are not religious, but seeing 'Holocaust' on television made me think."[38] In this new search for roots the young, many of whom were brought up in an atheistic environment, seemed to cling to anything that would satisfy the new thrist for Jewish authenticity. "Everyone creates his own manner of returning to Judaism; isolating oneself from it is a thing of the past," remarked the community organizer, Michel Kalef.[39]

The cultural, intellectual and religious revival touched various social and age groups, but seemed centered primarily on the young, the large segment of those under thirty who make up almost a third of the 700,000-strong French Jewish community.[40] Although not constituting a majority, those searching for links to Judaism were predominantly the educated, who were eager to discover a heritage to which they were never exposed. "We are witnessing an in-depth, qualitative revitalization," wrote a French sociologist.[41] The success in consolidating and expanding this nucleus will determine to a great extent the future vitality of French Jewry.

On the religious level there have also been significant changes. Observance of Kashrut and a stricter adherence to Halacha represented external signs of a deeper change. In 1982, the Paris region had close to twenty Kosher restaurants; in 1955 there were only four.[42] Microphones and organs have been banned in many synagogues and young Rabbis with traditional Yeshiva training assumed pulpits in large congregations. The possibility of a synthesis of divergent Judaic traditions was demonstrated by the "Lubavitch" organization, a Hassidic movement originating in Eastern Europe, which had remarkable success in recruiting to its ranks hundreds of North African Jews. By 1983, the vast majority of the 14,000 children in day schools were receiving an Orthodox education.

The wave of socio-cultural and religious rejuvenation is not devoid of some factors that put the soundness of the experience, as well as its future, into question. Not only is the majority left untouched by the educational immersion process, but two-thirds of French Jewry remain without any link to communal organizations.[43] An official of the community lamented the fact that one "rarely sees the masses" involved in the Jewish community.[44] The intermarriage rate in this segment was, in 1981, close to 50% (the rate for those in contact with the community was 35%).[45] In spite of the deepening religious involvement of a substantial minority, erosion of religion continues. The Chief Rabbi, René Sirat, decried the "slow but dramatic dejudaization" of the majority.[46] He has claimed that the intermarriage rate stood at 70% and that 82% of the children received no Jewish education in any form.[47] As one critical observer noted, many are Jews on the street but have forgotten how to be Jewish at home, in ironic contrast to an earlier period.[48]

The transition from secular universalism to Jewish phenomenology, which is essentially religious, is not easily bridged and some of the solutions border on the frivolous. The leap from Mao and Lenin to the Talmud and Cabala had more than a touch of the exotic about it. A nostalgic plunge into the study of Yiddish or of Sephardism removed from their existential contexts, can at best lead to folklore. Some have suggested that the sudden thirst for Judaica was in itself a form of assimilation since it tended to imitate the Corsican or Breton plunge into ethnicity. Many of the young students of Yiddish were children of Communists who were distant from Judaism, and few of the aspiring Talmudists had a knowledge of Hebrew, although a serious study of the Talmud requires a background in rabbinic and Biblical texts. There was reason to wonder if this dipping into Judaic sources would, as with so many Parisian intellectual fashions, yield to more appealing new ideologies.

A by-product of the quest for new modes of Jewish identity was the emergence of a "neo-Diasporism" based on a rejection of the centrality of the State of Israel and the development of a culture centered on Diaspora history and on Yiddish. In 1975, Richard Marienstras, a Professor at the University of Paris, denounced the "myth" of the centrality of Israel which, in his view, not only negates a fundamental component of Jewish history, but also distracts the Diaspora from reflection on its philosophical and organizational problems.[49] Marienstras has argued that dispersion assures Jewish survival and that ingathering, on the contrary, endangers it.[50] He has called for the establishment of Jewish schools where the curriculum would be "historical, cultural and linguistic...and not traditionalist, Zionist or religious."[51] His programme also included a radical change in the structure of communal organizations and a diminution of the influence of Zionism and Israel.

Ignoring the fact that Diaspora-oriented Jewish culture has been a failure in the past, and that Jewish problems are essentially different from the preoccupations of such French regionalists as the Bretons, Marienstras sought a political alliance with the regionalists. He also disregarded the fact that the new regionalist culture, such as the Breton "Céltitude," was tainted with a certain Judeophobia. It is noteworthy that a Maghreb equivalent of neo-Diasporism, a sense of nostalgia for the North African ghetto, was echoed in the writings of the novelists Marco Koskas, Katia Rubinstein and Guy Sitbon.

In spite of the remarkable transformation in mentality in the last few years some French Jews continued to express forms of nineteenth-century Jewish ultra-patriotism and to view themselves as Frenchmen of the "Mosaic persuasion." In 1980, the writer Roger Stéphane insisted that, although a Jew, "he knows only one spirtual definition," that of France, "feels as French as any other Frenchman," and does not side "instinctively with Israel" whose fate he has as much at heart "as that of Czechoslovakia."[52] Such rejections of the notion of Jewish solidarity in the post-Holocaust period are absent in most other Western Diasporas. Moreover, in France, left-wing ideology and the irresistible pull of "Francité" (Frenchness), has led to some of the most extreme manifestations of secular Jewish, anti-Zionism. A writer who called himself "a free Jew" claimed that Zionists have become "persecutors."[53] Assimilationist sentiment has not disappeared. In 1978, 32% of French Jewry still wished to be referred to only as "Israélites,"[54] not by the more direct "Juif" preferred by the proud young generation. The "Israélites" still bear their Jewish identity discretely and tend to fix their "Mezuzot" inside their apartments and to drop their voice to a whisper when the "unwelcome" word "Juif" is uttered.[55]

The desire not be singled out, to melt into the mainstream of French society, continues to exercise a strong pull on a community that has repeatedly overestimated the weight of assimilation as a factor in eliminating anti-Semitism. In the past, these errors resulted in a paralysis that prevented effective responses to anti-Jewish hostility. To some extent, the tendency to discount the threat, to veil the unattractive aspects of French society and to stress its advantages and amenities, is still present. Writing about his congregants, the English-born Rabbi of a Paris synagogue has observed: "They respond to what I consider my sympathetic condemnation of France and French ways with a eulogy of the pleasures of life in France and the need to understand the French who, en fin de compte, are the 'nicest, kindest people — if a little egotistical'...and so on, and so on."[56] Even the Vichy experience, with all of its consequences, did not succeed in erasing this attitude. The former Chief Rabbi of France attempted to convince an interviewer that the resurgence of anti-Semitism in recent years had its source in the German occupation period: "without it all this racism would not occur."[57]

A well-known writer and publicist has called this attitude "blindness." Deploring the community's silence after the assassination in Paris of the controversial Jewish activist Pierre Goldman, Claude Lanzmann, echoing the views of historians who have accused French Jews of passivity in time of crises, castigated the "incurable blinders of my Jewish brothers," and addressed them with a plea: "when will you cease wishing to be respectable at all costs...[this is] a detestable attitude which forces us to face our killers in a disorganized fashion, when the cyclical crises return."[58] Other social critics have referred to this mentality as a "congenitally alienated and colonized psychology."[59] In the face of the mounting anti-Jewish violence in the late 1970s Shmuel Trigano wondered why the community has not prepared "an emergency plan," a "brain trust" that would "mobilize consciences and actions," and concluded that "the leadership of the Jewish community is absent."[60]

Weaknesses in communal structure also affect the Jewish renewal. Communal organizations have been accused, not without some justification, of constituting exclusive clubs reserved for the rich and for a few intellectual personalities. The traditional leadership has lacked, according to its critics, the kind of deep personal and financial commitment necessary for effective handling of basic problems. Hesitations have led to "an often fragile, ambiguous situation"[61] which has alientated the young.

The split is not limited to generational differences. There

seemed to be a clear lack of compatibility between the mostly upper-bourgeois, Parisian, Ashkenazic spokesmen for the community and the predominantly lower-middle class, suburban, young Sephardim, although a change in leadership has begun. The weakness of the communal organizations could also be attributed to the relatively small staff they employ. The much larger French community has only a tenth of the number of communal workers employed by British Jewry. The "Fonds Social Juif Unifié," which funds most of the educational and social institutions of the community, has only recently decided to create a training program to remedy this situation. Fund-raising, except for emergency relief drives for Israel, remains a formidable task.

Even the high-profile, militant "Renouveau Juif" movement was more symptomatic of a new climate than of a strengthened communal structure. While it has proven capable of bringing out tens of thousands for occasional day-long gatherings, "Renouveau Juif" has yet to demonstrate that it can exercise effective influence on day-to-day communal activity. There is no conclusive evidence that the "Jewish vote" it tried to mobilize in the 1981 Presidential election materialized to a significant degree. It is worth noting, however, that some of the most important, ground-breaking initiatives did not stem from the framework of existing organizations.

For the first time since emancipation French-Jewish masses are willing to affirm openly their Jewish identity, and it is evident that there exists a new dynamism ready to challenge the establishment. Nevertheless, rather than build a new ideological and political current, movements such as "Renouveau Juif" have capitalized on dissatisfaction with the existing leadership, on authentic popular sentiment against a communal organization that failed to address crucial problems in a manner dictated by new attitudes. The rebels will probably emerge as the future leaders of French Jewry, but it remains to be seen whether their youthful militancy can be translated into radically different political wisdom and moral leadership.

# Notes

[1]M. Williams, "French Jewry - a Personal View," *European Judaism*, no. 1 (1978), p. 6.

[2]*Essai sur la régénération physique, morale et politique des Juifs, 1789* (Paris: Editions d'Histoire Sociale, 1968), pp. 158, 134.

[3]Trigano, *La République et les Juifs*, p. 59.

[4]P. Hyman, *From Dreyfus to Vichy, The Remaking of French Jewry, 1906-1939* (New York: Columbia University Press, 1979), p. 2.

[5]Schnapper, *Jewish Identities in France*, p. 102.

[6]*Ibid.*, p. 118.

[7]S. Vormus, "Et si demain...," *Le Journal des communautés* (October, 1980), p. 8.

[8]Henri Raczymow, "Vous avez dit 'différent'?," *L'Arche* (Sept.-Oct., 1980), p. 93.

[9]*Le Monde*, October 25, 1980.

[10]In an interview with this writer in May, 1982.

[11]S. Schwarzfuchs, *L'Arche* (Sept.-Oct., 1980), p. 88.

[12]*Le Monde*, April 2, 1980.

[13]*Ibid.*, Jan. 29, 1977.

[14]Schnapper, *Jewish Identities in France*, pp. 100-101 (the original French edition, *Juifs et Israélites*, was published in 1980).

[15]*Ibid.*, p. 87.

[16]E. Deutsch, "Radiographie d'une communauté," *L'Arche* (Sept.-Oct., 1980), p. 83.

[17]*L'Arche* (Sept.-Oct., 1979), p. 68.

[18]*Ibid.*, p. 69.

[19]M. Abitbol, "Etre Juif et Français," *Jonathan*, no. 19 (April, 1984), p. 16.

[20]William Safran, "France and her Jews: from 'Culte Israélite' to 'Lobby Juif'," *The Tocqueville Review*, Vol. V, no. 1 (Spring-Summer, 1983), p. 120.

[21]Deutsch, *L'Arche* (Sept.-Oct., 1980), p. 81.

[22]Gérard Fellous, "Juifs entre eux," *Le Monde*, Aug. 5-6, 1984.

[23]Deutsch, *L'Arche* (Sept.-Oct., 1980), p. 80.

[24]A. Loss, *L'Arche* (Sept.-Oct., 1980), p. 59.

[25]Robert Badinter at a round-table discussion on "Jews in Public Life," held at the "Centre Poissonnière" in Paris, on June 2, 1981. Badinter served as Minister of Justice under Mitterrand from 1981 to 1986.

[26]André Wurmser at the June 2, 1981 debate on "Jews in Public Life" (see preceding note).

[27]Guy de Rothschild, *L'Arche* (November, 1980), p. 63.

[28]*Les Nouvelles littéraires*, Sept. 13-19, 1979.

[29]Pierre Dreyfus in Harris and Sédouy, *Juifs et Français*, p. 40.

[30]B.-H. Lévy, *Les Nouvelles littéraires*, Sept. 13-19, 1979.

[31]*Ibid.*

[32]Harris and Sédouy, *Juifs et Français*, p. 247.

[33]Schnapper, *Jewish Identities in France*, p. 102.

[34]Harris and Sédouy, *Juifs et Français*, p. 41.

[35]*L'Arche* (Sept.-Oct., 1980), p. 89.

[36]Schnapper, *Jewish Identities in France*, p. 11.

[37]L. Sichler, "Le Grand Rabbin qui vient du Sud," *L'Express*, June 21, 1980.

[38]*Ibid.*

[39]From a conversation with this author in Paris in June, 1981.

[40]According to a SOFRES poll taken in 1977. A socio-demographic survey conducted by the CNRS shows the figures to be from 577,000 to 720,000 (Harris and Sédouy, *Juifs et Français*, p. 9, n. 1).

[41]Deutsch, *L'Arche* (Sept.-Oct., 1980), p. 85.

[42]These figures were obtained from officials of CRIF in May, 1981.

[43]Deutsch, *L'Arche* (Sept.-Oct., 1980) pp. 80-81.

[44]N. Goldman, *L'Arche* (May, 1981), p. 52.

[45]*Ibid.*, pp. 83, 85.

[46]*Information juive* (April, 1981).

[47]In an interview he gave to the *Canadian Jewish News*, Nov. 3, 1983. The Chief Rabbi claimed that 8% attend Jewish day schools, a further 8% are exposed to other forms of Jewish education, and 2% are enrolled only in youth programmes and summer camps.

[48]Finkielkraut, *Le Juif imaginaire.*

[49]*Etre un peuple en diaspora* (Paris: Maspéro, 1975), p. 52.

[50]R. Marienstras, "La Minorité juive," *Combat pour la diaspora*, nos. 11-12 (1983), p. 122.

[51]*Ibid.*, p. 126.

[52]*Le Monde*, April 10, 1980.

[53]Rachline, *Un Juif libre*, p. 20.

[54]Williams, *European Judaism*, p. 6.

[55]*Ibid.*

[56]*Ibid.*, p. 7.

[57]Harris and Sédouy, *Juifs et Français*, p. 51.

[58]"Les Temps de la déraison," *Les Temps modernes* (October, 1980), p. 566.

[59]S. Trigano, "Face à la montée des périls," *L'Arche* (Sept.-Oct., 1979), p. 99.

[60]*Ibid.*, p. 101.

[61]H. Smolarski, *Tribune juive*, May 15-21, 1981.

# Epilogue

That the beginning of the regeneration of authentic Jewish identity in France should coincide with renewed concern over the rebirth of anti-Jewish sentiment may appear incongruous. It is indeed paradoxical that a community assimilation-bound for almost two centuries has revealed a depth of attachment to its ancestral heritage, one surprising to both friend and foe, precisely when it seemed on an irreversible path to religio-ethnic extinction.

Although heirs to one of the oldest and richest civilizations on earth, Jews have also suffered the status of an often despised and persecuted minority. Not surprisingly, many sought to escape their condition, to become part of the majority in their "host" societies. Across the centuries this assimilationist urge has resulted in conversions, abdications, moral suicides, betrayals and even adhesion to forces inimical to their own people. Whenever given the opportunity, many Jews strove to adhere to the dominant culture, for both practical reasons and out of an often-mistaken perception of security.

French Jews in particular, from the end of the eighteenth century, were provided with a new vehicle for assimilation in the guise of emancipation. The 1791 law of emancipation gave French Jewry the opportunity of integrating into French society without, it thought, needing to abandon its corporate adherence to Judaism. In reality, however, the caveats and limitations of the emancipatory path led to profound assimilation. Yet in a startling reversal of this historical process, in contemporary France mass assimilation is now coming to an end. The post-Holocaust birth of the State of Israel, delegitimation of traditional right-wing anti-Semitism, and the more recent onset of a crisis of faith in leftist, universalist ideologies, have together provided the framework for a rebirth of Jewish consciousness. The decline of ideologies which denounced the essence of Judaic thought, which were critical of Jewish loyalty and demanded the abandonment of a specifically Jewish identity as the price of acceptance, prompted a search for new truths and a new sense of self. To many young French Jews it came as a surprising, and reinforcing, revelation that Judaism contained within itself an appeal to a universalism more genuine than the one they had pursued in the name of Marxist and other secularist ideals.

This return to the Jewish heritage also coincided with the advent of a momentous challenge to France's long tradition of cultural centralization. The awakening of a regionalist quest for cultural and political independence reinforced the emerging belief among Jews that they too were entitled to preserve their cultural heritage while maintaining full rights as Frenchmen. No longer satisfied with their designation as "Frenchmen of the Mosaic persuasion," they demanded a form of cultural autonomy and legitimacy akin to that sought by the regionalists.

The "Jewish question" in France has, therefore, taken on unexpected dimensions. The quest for a new status has profound implications not only for French Jewry, but for French society as a whole. And the successful resolution of this challenge has direct bearing on some of France's most deeply-rooted socio-cultural and political problems. Recognition of the legitimacy of new Jewish aspirations would be a vindication of what is best in the French tradition of justice, equality, and affirmation of the nobility of the human spirit. It would be in harmony too with the legacy of that France which, in time of crisis over the "Jewish question," threw in its lot with the "Dreyfusards," with those who, like Emile Zola, incarnated a profoundly important "moment of conscience."

A nation which has struggled with itself for two centuries in order to fulfill the exalted ideals it bequeathed to the world may—precisely through a reorientation in attitudes towards its Jews—vanquish the obstacles which until now have impaired the realization of those ideals. By exorcizing the demons which have frustrated the achievement of the 1791 emancipation, by finally allowing its proclaimed magnanimity to achieve fruition, France will have finally come to grips with, and overcome, its old anti-Semitic temptations. Allowing Jews to remain faithful to their ancestral traditions even as they exercise in full their unconditional right to "francité," would resoundingly affirm the still-revolutionary promise of a truly human "Egalité."

The stakes posed by the present historical moment are indeed high, for French Jews, for other minorities, and for France generally. By resolving, once and for all, her "Jewish problem" in a direction consonant with her still-unrealized Revolutionary promise, France may well achieve a new, deeper sense of human community. In the long run, this can only mean the reinvigoration of her democratic, and national, foundations.

# Bibliography

## BOOKS

Aron, Raymond. *De Gaulle, Israël et les Juifs*. Paris: Plon, 1968.

Arvon, Henri. *Les Juifs et l'idéologie*. Paris: PUF, 1978.

Benoist, Alain de. *Les Idées de l'endroit*. Paris: Editions Libres Hallier, 1979.

Brunn, Julien. *La Nouvelle Droite*. Paris: Nouvelles Editions Oswald, 1979.

Cau, Jean. *Lettre ouverte à tout Le Monde*. Paris: Albin Michel, 1976.

Clément, Claude. *Israël et la Ve République*. Paris: Olivier Orban, 1978.

Cohen, Samy. *De Gaulle, les Gaullistes et Israël*. Paris: Alain Moreau, 1974.

Cohn, Norman. *Warrant for Genocide, The Myth of the Jewish World-Conspiracy and the Protocols of the Elders of Zion*. London: Eyre and Spottiswoode, 1967.

Crosbie, Sylvia K. *A Tacit Alliance: France and Israel from Suez to the Six Day War*. Princeton, N.J.: Princeton University Press, 1974.

Dan, Uri. *L'Embargo*. Paris: Editions Premières, 1969.

Dawidowicz, Lucy. *The Jewish Presence*. New York: Holt, Rinehart and Winston, 1977.

Fabre-Luce, Alfred. *Journal de France, Mars 1939-Juillet 1940*. Paris: Imprimerie de Trévoux, 1940.

Fabre-Luce, Alfred. *Pour en finir avec l'antisémitisme*. Paris: Julliard, 1979.

Finkielkraut, Alain. *Le Juif imaginaire*. Paris: Seuil, 1980.

Finkielkraut, Alain. *La Réprobation d'Israël*. Paris: Denoël-Gonthier, 1983.

Freiberg, J.W. *The French Press, Class, State and Ideology*. New York: Praeger, 1981.

Friedländer, Saul. *L'Antisémitisme nazi*. Paris: Seuil, 1971.

Furet, François. *L'Atelier de l'histoire*. Paris: Flammarion, 1982.

Givet, Jacques. *Israël et le génocide inachevé*. Paris: Plon, 1979.

Grégoire, Henri (Abbé). *Essai sur la régénération physique, morale et politique des juifs, 1789*. Paris: Editions d'Histoire Sociale, 1968.

Guedj, Aimé and Jacques Girault. *"Le Monde"... humanisme, objectivité et politique*. Paris: Editions Sociales, 1970.

Harris, André and Alain de Sédouy. *Juifs et Français*. Paris: Grasset, 1979.

Hay, Malcolm. *Europe and the Jews*. Boston: Beacon Press, 1961.

Hermone, Jacques. *La Gauche, Israël et les Juifs*. Paris: La Table Ronde, 1970.

Hyman Paula. *From Dreyfus to Vichy, The Remaking of French Jewry, 1906-1939*. New York: Columbia University Press, 1979.

Jeanneney, Jean-Noël and Jacques Julliard. *"Le Monde" de Beuve-Méry ou le métier d'Alceste*. Paris: Seuil, 1979.

Jobert, Michel. *L'Autre regard*. Paris: Grasset, 1976.

Katz, Jacob. *From Prejudice to Destruction, Anti-Semitism, 1700-1933*. Cambridge: Harvard University Press, 1980.

Kolodziej, Edward J. *French International Policy Under De Gaulle and Pompidou.* Ithaca and London: Cornell University Press, 1974.

Kriegel, Annie. *Communismes au miroir français.* Paris: Gallimard, 1974.

Kriegel, Annie. *Israël est-il coupable?* Paris: Laffont, 1982.

Lapierre, Jean W. *L'Information sur l'Etat d'Israël dans les grands quotidiens français en 1958.* Paris: CNRS, 1968.

Legris, Michel. *"Le Monde" tel qu'il est.* Paris: Plon, 1976.

Lévy, Bernard-Henri. *L'Idéologie française.* Paris: Grasset, 1981.

Malino, Frances and Bernard Wasserstein, eds. *The Jews in Modern France.* Hanover and London: University Press of New England, 1985.

Mandel, Arnold. *Nous autres Juifs.* Paris: Hachette, 1978.

Marienstras, Richard. *Etre un peuple en diaspora.* Paris: Maspéro, 1975.

Marrus, Michael R. and Robert O. Paxton. *Vichy France and the Jews.* New York: Basic Books, 1981.

Maurras, Charles. *Dictionnaire politique et critique.* Paris: La Cité des Libres, 1932.

Mehlman, Jeffrey. *Legacies of Anti-Semitism in France.* Minneapolis: University of Minnesota Press, 1983.

Morin, Edgar. *La Rumeur d'Orléans.* Paris: Seuil, 1969.

Noël, Léon. *Comprendre De Gaulle.* Paris: Plon, 1972.

Plumyène, Jean and Raymond Lasierra. *Les Fascismes français, 1923-1963.* Paris: Seuil, 1963.

Poliakov, Léon. *De l'antisionisme à l'antisémitisme.* Paris: Calmann-Lévy, 1969.

Poliakov, Léon. *De Moscou à Beyrouth.* Paris: Calmann-Lévy, 1983.

Pons, Gregory. *Les Rats noirs.* Paris: J.-C. Simoën, 1977.

Rabi, Wladimir. *Un Peuple de trop sur la terre?.* Paris: Les Presses d'Aujourd'hui, 1979.

Rachline, Michel. *Un Juif libre.* Paris: Guy Authier, 1976.

Rouanet, Pierre. *Pompidou.* Paris: Grasset, 1969.

Saint-Robert, Philippe de. *Les Septennats interrompus.* Paris: Laffont, 1977.

Sartre, Jean-Paul. *Réflexions sur la question juive.* Paris: Gallimard, 1954.

Schnapper, Dominique. *Jewish Identities in France, An Analysis of Contemporary French Jewry.* Chicago and London: University of Chicago Press, 1983.

Serant, Paul. *Les Dissidents de l'Action Française.* Paris: Editions Copernic, 1978.

Simonnot, Philippe. *"Le Monde" et le pouvoir.* Paris: Les Presses d'Aujourd'hui, 1977.

Sternhell, Zeev. *La Droite révolutionnaire, 1885-1914, les origines françaises du Fascisme.* Paris: Seuil, 1978.

Thibau, Jacques. *"Le Monde", histoire d'un journal, un journal dans l'histoire.* Paris: J.-C. Simoën, 1978.

Toussenel, Alphonse de. *Les Juifs rois de l'époque, histoire de la féodalité financière.* Paris: Librairie de l'Ecole Sociétaire, 1845.

Trigano, Shmuel. *La République et les Juifs.* Paris: Les Presses d'Aujourd'hui, 1982.

Vacher de Lapouge, Georges. *L'Aryen et son rôle social.* Paris: Albert Fontemoing, 1899.

Wajsman, Patrick and R.-F. Teissèdre. *Nos politiciens face au conflit israélo-arabe.* Paris: Fayard, 1969.

Weber, Eugen. *National Revival in France, 1905-1914.* Berkeley: University of California Press, 1959.

Winock, Michel. *Edouard Drumont et Cie, antisémitisme et fascisme en France.* Paris: Seuil, 1982.

Wistrich, Robert S. *The Left Against Zion.* London: Vallentine, 1979.

Wurmser, André. *Fidèlement votre.* Paris: Grasset, 1979.

# ARTICLES

Abitbol, Michel. "Etre Juif et Français." *Jonathan*, (Montreal), no. 19 (April, 1984), 15-20.

Bauer, Yehuda. "Anti-Semitism Today — A Fact or a Fiction?." *Midstream*, vol XXX, no. 8, (October, 1984), 24-31.

Bénichou, Paul. "Sur quelques sources françaises de l'antisémitisme moderne." *Commentaire*, no. 1 (1978), 67-79.

Bloch-Michel, Jean. "Anti-Semitism and the French 'New Right'," *Dissent* (1980), 291-298.

"Dérapage de la gauche?." (Interviews with B. Barret-Kriegel, E. Le Roy Ladurie, D. Lindenberg and P.-A. Taguieff). *Les Nouveaux cahiers*, no. 71 (Winter, 1982-1983), 9-22.

Higonnet, Patrice. "On the extent of Anti-Semitism in Modern France." in F. Malino and B. Wasserstein, eds. *The Jews in Modern France*. Hanover and London: University Press of New England, 1985, 207-212.

Krantz, Frederick. "Response to M. Marrus." *Middle East Focus*, Vol. VII, no. 1 (May, 1984), 20-23.

Landes, David. "Two Cheers for Emancipation." in F. Malino and B. Wasserstein, eds. *The Jew in Modern France*. Hanover and London: University Press of New England, 1985, 228-309.

Marienstras, Richard. "La Minorité juive." *Combat pour la diaspora*, nos. 11-12 (1983).

Marrus, Michael R. "Are the French Anti-Semitic?" *Jerusalem Quarterly*, no. 32 (Summer, 1984), 81-97.

Marrus, Michael R. "Is There a New Anti-Semitism? *"Middle East Focus*, Vol. VI, no. 1 (November, 1983), pp. 13-16; 32.

Rebatet, Lucien. "D'un Céline l'autre." *L.-F. Céline, Cahiers de l'herne*, no. 6 (1972), 42-55.

Safran, William. "France and her Jews: From 'Culte Israélite' to 'Lobby Juif'." *The Tocqueville Review*, Vol. V, no. 1 (Spring-Summer, 1983), 101-135.

Samuels, Shimon. "Anti-Semitism in France: Roots and Consequences." *ADL International Report*. (June, 1980).

Trigano, Shmuel. "From Individual to Collectivity: The Rebirth of the 'Jewish Nation' in France." in F. Malino and B. Wasserstein, eds. *The Jews in Modern France*. Hanover and London: University Press of New England, 1985, 245-281.

Walker, Gila. "Divided They Stand." *The B'nai Brith International Jewish Monthly* (March, 1983).

Weinberg, Henry H. "*Le Monde* and Israel." *Middle East Focus*, Vol. III, no. 6 (March, 1981), 14-17.

Weinberg, Henry H. "French Jewry: Trauma and Renewal." *Midstream*, Vol. XXVIII, no. 10 (December, 1982), 7-12.

Weinberg, Henry H. "French Jewry in Transition." *Proceedings of the Western Society for French History*, Vol. IX, Lawrence, Kansas: University of Kansas Press, 1982, 414-423.

Weinberg, Henry H. "The Image of the Jew in Late Nineteenth-Century French Literature." *Jewish Social Studies*, Vol. XLV, Nos. 3-4 (Summer-Fall, 1983), 241-50.

Weinberg, Henry H. "French Jewry under the Mitterrand Presidency." *Contemporary French Civilization*, Vol. VIII, Nos. 1-2 (Fall-Winter, 1983-84), 228-41.

Weinberg, Henry H. "Facing the Left and the Right in France." *Midstream*, Vol.

XXXI, no. 3 (March, 1985), 3-6.

White, S. "The Conclave at 'Le Monde'." *The Spectator* (March 1, 1980).

Williams, Michael. "French Jewry - a Personal view." *European Judaism*, no. 1 (1978), 5-7.

Wistrich, Robert S. "The Anti-Zionist Masquerade." *Midstream*, Vol, XXIX, no. 7 (August-September, 1983), 8-18.

## PERIODICALS

This section includes dailies, weeklies, monthlies and quarterlies which constitute most of the primary sources. References to items drawn from most of these periodicals appear in the notes only.

### DAILY NEWSPAPERS
*Combat*
*Le Figaro*
*The Globe and Mail*
*L'Humanité*
*Libération*
*Le Matin*
*Le Monde*
*The New York Times*
*Le Quotidien de Paris*
*The Times* (London)

### WEEKLIES
*Le Carnard enchaîné*
*L'Express*
*Le Figaro-magazine*
*The Jewish Chronicle* (London)
*The New York Times Magazine*
*Le Nouvel observateur*
*Les Nouvelles littéraires*
*Le Point*
*Tribune juive*

### MONTHLIES AND QUARTERLIES
*L'Arche*
*Art press international*
*Le Droit de vie*
*Eléments*
*Esprit*
*Information juive*
*Le Journal des communautés*
*Les Nouveaux cahiers*
*Les Temps modernes*
*La Terre retrouvée*
*Traces*

# Index